FORGIVENESS

A Guide for Prayer

by
Jacqueline Syrup Bergan
S. Marie Schwan

Take and Receive series

Saint Mary's Press
Christian Brothers Publications
Winona, Minnesota

Companion books are available in this Take and Receive series. Write to
    Saint Mary's Press
    Terrace Heights
    Winona, MN 55987

All scriptural excerpts are from *The Jerusalem Bible*, Copyright © 1966, by Darton, Longman & Todd, Limited, Doubleday & Company, Inc., used with permission of the publisher.

Selections from *The Scriptural Exercises of St. Ignatius*, translated by David L. Fleming, S.J. (The Institute of Jesuit Sources, St. Louis, 1978), are reprinted with permission.

With special thanks to our typist, S. Christine Johnson, and to S. Doreen Charest, proofreader.

Printed in the United States of America

Printing—sixth fifth
    1993 92 91 90 89

ISBN 0-88489-169-0

To my mother and father
Agnes Deschenes Syrup
Lloyd Elmer Syrup

— Jackie

To my mother and father
Amanda Martell Schwan
Jerome J. Schwan

— Marie

CONTENTS

FOREWORD

St. John writes: "If we say, 'We are free of the guilt of sin,' we deceive ourselves; the truth is not to be found in us. But if we acknowledge our sins, he who is just can be trusted to forgive our sins and cleanse us from every wrong" (1 John 1:8-9).

Forgiveness, the second volume of the series Take and Receive, is—like the first volume, *Love*—a guide for prayer based on the word of God. It will enable us by God's grace not only to face our sinfulness in a calm and hopeful way, but also to seek God's forgiveness through Jesus Christ who "is an offering for our sins" (1 John 2:2). In other words, this book is a guide to peace through reconciliation with God.

Because it flows out of the word of God, this guide is for every Christian who longs to die to sin and to live for God in Christ Jesus (Rom. 6:11). My prayer is that everyone who uses this book will come to believe and to experience that "it is in Christ and through his blood that we have been redeemed and our sins forgiven, so immeasurably generous is God's favor to us" (Eph. 1:7-8).

+ Victor H. Balke
Bishop of Crookston

December 31, 1984

COVER DESIGN

For see, the winter is past
the rains are over and gone.
The flowers appear on the earth.
The season of glad songs has come,
the cooing of the turtledove
is heard in our land.   Sg. 2:11-12

A "season of glad songs has" begun; throughout the Church is heard the murmur of prayer. Quietly, and in stillness, within the hearts of Christians everywhere, winter has given way to the vitality of spring — the coming of the Spirit.

Among the heralds of spring is the return and nesting of birds. From the days of ancient Israel even to our own times, birds have been symbolic, not only of our deep homing instincts, but also of our creative impulse, and of our desire for transcendence.

There are frequent allusions to doves throughout the scriptures. In the Song of Songs the dove announces spring; in Genesis the olive-bearing dove indicates the end of the flood (Gn. 8:11). At the Baptism of Jesus, the presence of the dove initiates a new age of the Spirit (Mk. 1:6).

As the pair of doves on the cover of volume one symbolized God's call to love, the cover of volume two symbolizes the blessing and nurturing of God's unconditional and forgiving love.

The mourning dove calls:

Come then, my love . . . for see, winter is past.

Sg. 2:10-11

The cover was designed by Donna Pierce Campbell, popular Minnesota artist, whose beauty and freshness of style mirrors the Spirit of renewal that this guide for prayer hopes to serve.

INTRODUCTION

This guide for prayer was inspired by the spiritual hunger we witnessed during the past years as we conducted parish days of renewal throughout northwestern Minnesota

People shared with us their need and eagerness for guidance and support in developing a personal relationship with God. Gradually we grew in the awareness that for too long the laity has been deprived of resources that are an integral part of the tradition of spirituality within the Church.

One treasure, within this tradition, is the Spiritual Exercises of St. Ignatius. The Exercises were a response to the need of the laity in the 16th century, and have only recently been discovered anew. In the light of Vatican II, with its emphasis on scripture, interior renewal and the emergence of the laity, the Exercises have received a new relevance.

As we endeavored to adapt the pattern of the Exercises to parish days of renewal, we discovered an approach for integrating personal prayer with life circumstances that is appropriate to the needs, language and lifestyle of the laity.

Forgiveness: A Guide for Prayer is the second of five projected volumes in the series Take and Receive. Each of these books will provide a series of scripture passages with commentaries and suggested approaches to prayer. The theme of each volume will directly correlate with a segment of the Exercises, though each book can be used independently of the others.

The first volume of the series, *Love: A Guide for Prayer*, made use of the themes present in the Principle and Foundation of the Spiritual Exercises. Those themes were the affirmation of human creaturehood, indifference to all created things, and commitment. The book centered on God's love, our total dependence on His love and the call to respond in freedom to praise, reverence and serve God.

The second volume, *Forgiveness*, correlates with the first week of the Spiritual Exercises of St. Ignatius. The theme treats personal and collective sinfulness insofar as it is an obstacle to the receiving of God's love. Sin and sinner are considered in light of God's merciful and forgiving love.

ix

To confront one's own sinfulness is an extremely painful process. In the tradition of St. Ignatius, the passages and prayer approaches devoted to this theme are very direct. A segment of the guide is focused on looking at various sinful tendencies to discover one's own area of sinfulness. The grace prayed for frequently is for shame and for a deepening sorrow for one's sinfulness. The shame ought not to be confused with an unhealthy guilt, but is better interpreted as a self-conscious awareness of the disorder and selfishness that permeates one's attitudes and/or behavior. (24, p. 252*)

In addition, three of the days are spent contemplating the horrible possibility of hell.

Due to the nature of these meditations/contemplations, we encourage those who make serious use of this book to consider arranging for a spiritual companion who can offer wisdom and support at the difficult times, should they arise.

The guide concludes with a segment on the call of Christ and our response.

Written specifically as a support for solitary prayer, the guide can also serve as a resource for faith-sharing in small groups.

The series of guides makes no claim to be the Spiritual Exercises, nor to be a commentary on them. It is an attempt to make available a means of entering into the Christocentric dynamic of conversion found in the Exercises.

In committing this approach of prayer to writing, it is our hope that more people will be able to draw nourishment from the word of God, experience God's unique love for them, and become aware of the particular intention God holds for each of them.

While we have attempted to be sensitive to the use of inclusive language in the commentaries and approaches to prayer, we have not been entirely consistent. We have been reluctant to make changes in the biblical text out of respect, not only for the word of God, but also for those people who may find these changes offensive.

Our prayer for those who use this guide is that they will be led by the spirit of Jesus into true spiritual freedom.

* Numbers keyed to Bibliography, pp. 163-166.

*May the God of our Lord Jesus Christ, the
Father of glory, give you a spirit of wisdom and
perception of what is revealed, to bring you to full
knowledge of him. May he enlighten the eyes of your
mind so that you can see what hope his call holds for
you, what rich glories he has promised the saints will
inherit and how infinitely great is the power that he
has exercised for us believers.*   Eph. 1:17-19

Jacqueline Syrup Bergan
S. Marie Schwan

The first Sunday of Advent, 1984

ORIENTATIONS

Lord, teach us to pray. Lk. 11:1

Prayer is our personal response to God's presence. We approach Him reverently with a listening heart. He speaks first. In prayer, we acknowledge His presence and in gratitude respond to Him in love. The focus is always on God and on what He does.

The following suggestions are offered as ways of supporting and enabling attentiveness to God's word and our unique response:

A. Daily Pattern of Prayer

For each period of prayer, use the following pattern:

1. PREPARATION:
    + Plan to spend at least twenty minutes to one hour in prayer daily. Though there is nothing "sacred" about sixty minutes, most people find that an hour better provides for the quieting of self, the entrance into the passage, etc.
    + The evening before, take time to read the commentary as well as the scripture passage for the following day. Just before falling asleep, recall the scripture passage.

2. STRUCTURE OF THE PRAYER PERIOD:
    + Quiet yourself; be still inside and out. Relax. Breathe in deeply, hold your breath to the count of four, then exhale slowly through your mouth. Repeat several times.
    + Realize you are nothing without God; declare your dependency on Him.
    + Ask Him for the grace you want and need.
    + Read and reflect on your chosen scripture passage, using the appropriate form, e.g., meditation for poetic and non-story passages, contemplation for story / event passages, etc. See: Various Forms of Solitary Prayer, p. 2.
    + Close the prayer period with a time of conversation with Jesus and His Father. Speak and listen. Conclude with an Our Father.

1

3. REVIEW OF PRAYER: The review of prayer is a reflection at the con-
clusion of the prayer period. The purpose of the review is to heighten our awareness of how God has been present to us during the prayer period.

The review focuses primarily on the interior movements of consolation and desolation as they are revealed in our feelings of joy, peace, sadness, fear, ambivalence, anger, etc.

Often it is in the review that we become aware of how God has responded to our request for a particular grace.

Writing the review provides for personal accountability, and is a precious record of our spiritual journey. To write the review is a step toward self integration.

In the absence of a spiritual director or a spiritual companion the writing helps fill the need for evaluation and clarification. If one has a spiritual director, the written review offers an excellent means of preparing to share one's prayer experience.

Method: In a notebook or journal, after each prayer period, indicate the date and the passage. Answer each of the following questions:
+ Was there any word or phrase that particularly struck you?
+ What were your feelings? Were you peaceful? . . . loving? . . . trust-ing? . . . sad? . . . discouraged? . . . What do these feelings say to you?
+ How are you more aware of God's presence?
+ Is there some point to which it would be helpful to return in your next prayer period?

B. Various Forms of Solitary Prayer

There are various forms of scriptural prayer. Different forms appeal to dif-ferent people. Eventually, by trying various methods, we become adept at using approaches that are appropriate to particular passages and are in harmony with our personality and needs.

This guide will make use of the following forms:

1. MEDITATION: In meditation one approaches the scripture passage like a love letter; this approach is especially helpful in

praying poetic passages.

Method:
+ Read the passage slowly, aloud or in a whisper, letting the words wash over you, savoring them.
+ Stay with the words that especially catch your attention; absorb them the way the thirsty earth receives the rain.
+ Keep repeating a word or phrase, aware of the feelings that are awakened.
+ Read, and reread the passage lovingly as you would a letter from a dear friend, or as you would softly sing the chorus of a song.

2. CONTEMPLATION: In contemplation, we enter into a life event or story passage of scripture. We enter into the passage by way of imagination, making use of all our senses.

Theologians tell us that through contemplation we are able to "recall and be present at the mysteries of Christ's life" (23, p. 149).

The Spirit of Jesus, present within us through Baptism, teaches us, just as Jesus taught the apostles. The Spirit recalls and enlivens the particular mystery into which we enter through prayer. Just as in the Eucharist the Risen Jesus makes present the paschal mystery, in contemplation He brings forward the particular event we are contemplating and presents Himself within that mystery.

Method:
In contemplation, one enters the story as if one were there:
+ Watch what happens; listen to what is being said.
+ Become part of the mystery; assume the role of one of the persons.
+ Look at each of the individuals; what does he / she experience? To whom does each one speak?
+ What difference does it make for my life, my family, for society, if I hear the message?
In the Gospel stories, enter into dialogue with Jesus:
+ **Be there** with Him and for Him.
+ **Want Him,** hunger for Him.
+ **Listen** to Him.

3

+ **Let Him** be for you what He wants to be.
+ **Respond to Him.** (31, pp. 5-6)

3. CENTERING PRAYER: *"In centering prayer we go beyond thought and image, beyond the senses and the rational mind to that center of our being where God is working a wonderful work"* (56, p. 18).

Centering prayer is a very simple, pure form of prayer, frequently without words; it is an opening of our hearts to the Spirit dwelling within us.

In centering prayer, we spiral down into the deepest center of ourselves. It is the point of stillness within us where we most experience being created by a loving God who is breathing us into life. To enter into centering prayer requires a recognition of our dependency on God and a surrender to His Spirit of love.

". . . the Spirit too comes to help us in our weakness . . . the Spirit expresses our plea in a way that could never be put into words . . ." (Rm. 8:26).

The Spirit of Jesus within us cries out *"Abba, Father"* (Rm. 8:15).

Method: *"Pause a while and know that I am God"* (Ps. 46:10).
+ Sit quietly, comfortable and relaxed.
+ Rest within your longing and desire for God.
+ Move to the center within your deepest self. This movement can be facilitated by imaging yourself slowly descending in an elevator, or walking down flights of stairs, or descending a mountain, or going down into the water, as in a deep pool.
+ In the stillness, become aware of God's presence; peacefully absorb His love.

4. MANTRA: One means of centering prayer is the use of the "mantra" or "prayer word." The mantra can be a single word or a phrase. It may be a word from scripture or one that arises spontaneously from within your heart. The word or phrase represents, for you, the fullness of God.

Variations of the mantra may include the name "Jesus" or what is known as the Jesus prayer, "Lord, Jesus Christ, Son of the living God, have mercy on me, a sinner."

Method: The word or phrase is repeated slowly within oneself in harmony with one's breathing. For example, the first part of the Jesus prayer is said while inhaling; the second half, while exhaling.

4

5. MEDITATIVE READING: *"I opened my mouth; he gave me the scroll to eat and said, '. . . feed and be satisfied by the scroll I am giving you.' I ate it, and it tasted sweet as honey"* (Ez. 3:2-3).

One of the approaches to prayer is a reflective reading of scripture or other spiritual writings.

Spiritual reading is always enriching to our life of prayer. The method described below is especially supportive in times when prayer is difficult or dry.

Method: The reading is done slowly, pausing periodically to allow the words and phrases to enter within you. When a thought resonates deeply, stay with it, allowing the fullness of it to penetrate your being. Relish the word received. Respond authentically and spontaneously as in a dialogue.

6. JOURNALING: *"If you read my words, you will have some idea of the depths that I see in the mystery of Christ"* (Eph. 3:4).

Journaling is meditative writing. When we place pen on paper, spirit and body cooperate to release our true selves.

There is a difference between journaling and keeping a journal.

To journal is to experience ourselves in a new light as expression is given to the fresh images which emerge from our subconscious. Journaling requires putting aside preconceived ideas and control.

Meditative writing is like writing a letter to one we love. Memories are recalled, convictions are clarified and affections well up within us. In writing we may discover that emotions are intensified and prolonged.

Because of this, journaling can also serve in identifying and healing hidden, suppressed emotions such as anger, fear and resentment.

Finally, journaling can give us a deeper appreciation for the written word as we encounter it in scripture.

Method: There are many variations for the use of journaling in prayer. Among them are the following:

a. writing a letter addressed to God;

b. writing a conversation between oneself and another; the other may be Jesus, or another significant person. The dialogue can also be with an event, an

5

experience or a value. For example, death, separation or wisdom receives personal attributes and is imaged as a person with whom one enters into conversation;

c. writing an answer to a question, e.g., *"What do you want me to do for you?"* (Mk. 10:51) or *"Why are you weeping?"* (Jn. 20:15)

d. allowing Jesus or another scripture person to "speak" to us through the pen.

7. REPETITION: *"I will remain quietly meditating upon the point in which I have found what I desire without any eagerness to go on till I have been satisfied."* — St. Ignatius of Loyola (72, p. 110)

Repetition is the return to a previous period of prayer for the purpose of allowing the movements of God to deepen within one's heart.

Through repetitions, we fine-tune our sensitivities to God and to how He speaks in our prayer and within our life circumstances. The prayer of repetition allows for the experience of integrating who we are with who God is revealing Himself to be for us.

Repetitions are a way of honoring God's word to us in the earlier prayer period. It is recalling and pondering an earlier conversation with one we love. It is as if we say to God, "Tell me that again; what did I hear you saying?"

In this follow-up conversation or repetition we open ourselves to a healing presence that often transforms whatever sadness and confusion may have been experienced in the first prayer.

In repetitions, not only is the consolation (joy, warmth, peace) deepened, but the desolation (pain, sadness, confusion) is frequently brought to a new level of understanding and acceptance within God's plan for us.

Method: The period of prayer that we select to repeat is one in which we have experienced a significant movement of joy or sadness or confusion. It may also be a period in which nothing seemed to happen, due, perhaps, to our own lack of readiness at the time.

+ Recall the feelings of the first period of prayer.
+ Use, as a point of entry, the scene, word or feeling that was previously most significant.
+ Allow the Spirit to direct the inner movements of your heart during this time of prayer.

C. Spiritual Practices and Helps

1. EXAMEN OF CONSCIOUSNESS: *"Yahweh, you examine me and know me . . ."* (Ps. 139:1).

The examen of consciousness is the instrument by which we discover how God has been present to us and how we have responded to His presence through the day.

St. Ignatius believed this practice was so important that, in the event it was impossible to have a formal prayer period, he insisted that the examen would sustain one's vital link with God.

The examen of consciousness is not to be confused with an examination of conscience in which penitents are concerned with their failures. It is, rather, an exploration of how God is present within the events, circumstances, feelings of our daily lives.

What the review is to the prayer period, the examen is to our daily life. The daily discipline of an authentic practice of the examen effects the integrating balance which is essential for growth in relationship to God, to self, and to others.

The method reflects the "dynamic movement of personal love: what we always want to say to a person whom we truly love in the order in which we want to say it. . . . Thank you. . . . Help me. . . . I love you. . . . I'm sorry. . . . Be with me." (19, pp. 34-35)

> **Method:** The following prayer is a suggested approach to examen. The written response can be incorporated into the prayer journal.
>
> + God, my Father, I am totally dependent on you. Everything is gift from you. **All is gift.** I give you thanks and praise for the gifts of this day. . . .
> + Lord, I believe you work through and in time to reveal me to myself. Please give me an increased awareness of how you are guiding and shaping my life, as well as a more sensitive awareness of the obstacles I put in your way.
> + You have been present in my life today. Be near, now, as I reflect on:
> your presence in the **events** of today . . .
> your presence in the **feelings** I experienced today . . .
> your **call** to me . . .
> my **response** to you. . . .

+ Father, I ask your loving forgiveness and healing. The particular event of this day that I most want healed is. . . .

+ Filled with hope and a firm belief in your love and power, I entrust myself to your care, and strongly affirm. . . . (Claim the gift you most desire, most need; believe that God desires to give you that gift.)

2. FAITH-SHARING: *"Where two or three meet in my name, I shall be there with them"* (Mt. 18:20).

In the creation of community it is essential that members communicate intimately with each other about the core issues of their lives. For the Christian, this is faith sharing, and is an extension of daily solitary prayer.

A faith-sharing group is not a discussion group, not a sensitivity session, nor a social gathering. Members do not come together to share and receive intellectual or theological insights. Nor is the purpose of faith sharing the accomplishment of some predetermined task.

The purpose of faith sharing is to listen and to be open to God as He continues to reveal Himself in the Church community represented in the small group which comes together in His name. The fruit of faith sharing is the "building up" of the Church, the Body of Christ (Eph. 4:12).

The approach to faith sharing is one of reading and reflecting together on the word of God. Faith sharing calls us to share with each other, out of our deepest center, what it means to be a follower of Christ in our world today. To authentically enter into faith sharing is to come to know and love each other in Christ whose Spirit is the bonding force of community.

An image that faith-sharing groups may find helpful is that of a pool into which pebbles are dropped. The group gathers in a circle imaging themselves around a pool. Like a pebble being gently dropped into the water, each one offers a reflection — his/her "word" from God. In the shared silence, each offering is received. As the water ripples in concentric circles toward the outer reaches of the pool, so too this word enlarges and embraces, in love, each member of the circle.

Method: A group of seven to ten members gathers at a prearranged time and place.

- + The leader calls the group to prayer and invites them to some moments of silent centering, during which they pray for the presence of the Holy Spirit.
- + The leader gathers their silent prayer in an opening prayer, spontaneous or prepared.
- + One of the members reads a previously chosen scripture passage on which participants have spent some time in solitary prayer.
- + A period of silence follows each reading of the scripture.
- + The leader invites each one to share a word or phrase from the reading.
- + Another member rereads the passage; this is followed by a time of silence.
- + The leader invites those who wish, to share simply how this passage personally addresses them, e.g., challenging, comforting, inviting, etc.
- + Again the passage is read.
- + Members are invited to offer their spontaneous prayer to the Lord.
- + The leader draws the time of faith sharing to closure with a prayer, a blessing, an Our Father, or a hymn.
- + Before the group disbands, the passage for the following session is announced.

3. THE ROLE OF IMAGINATION IN PRAYER:

Imagination is our power of memory and recall which makes it possible for us to enter into the experience of the past and to create the future. Through images we are able to touch the center of who we are and to surface and give life and expression to the innermost levels of our being.

The use of images is important to our psycho-spiritual development. Images simultaneously reveal multiple levels of meaning and are therefore symbolic of our deeper reality.

Through the structured use of active imagination, we release the hidden energy and potential for wholeness which is already present within us.

When active imagination is used in the context of prayer, and **with an attitude of faith**, we open ourselves to the power and mystery of God's transforming presence wihin us.

Because scripture is, for the most part, a collection of stories and rich in sensual imagery, the use of active imagination in praying scripture is particularly enriching.

Through imaging scripture we go beyond the truth of history to discover the truth of the mystery of God's creative word in our lives (21, p. 76).

4. COPING WITH DISTRACTIONS

It is important not to become overly concerned or discouraged by distractions during prayer. Simply put them aside and return to your prayer material. If and when a distraction persists, it may be a call to attend prayerfully to the object of the distraction. For example, it would not be surprising if an unresolved conflict continues to surface until it has been dealt with.

Lord my God, when Your love spilled over
into creation
You thought of me.
I am
from love   of love   for love.

Let my heart, O God, always
recognize,
cherish,
and enjoy your goodness in all of creation.

Direct all that is me toward your praise.
Teach me reverence for every person, all things.
Energize me in your service.

Lord God
may nothing ever distract me from your
love . . .
neither health nor sickness
wealth nor poverty
honor nor dishonor
long life nor short life.

May I never seek nor choose to be other
than You intend or wish.   Amen.

called out of darkness

ROMANS 5:6-11

*We were still helpless when at his appointed moment Christ
died for sinful [humanity]. It is not easy to die even for a good
[person] — though of course for someone really worthy, [one]
might be prepared to die — but what proves that God loves
us is that Christ died for us while we were still sinners. Having
died to make us righteous, is it likely that he would now fail to
save us from God's anger? When we were reconciled to God by
the death of his Son, we were still enemies; now that we have
been reconciled, surely we may count on being saved by the
life of his Son? Not merely because we have been reconciled
but because we are filled with joyful trust in God, through
our Lord Jesus Christ, through whom we have already gained
our reconciliation.*

COMMENTARY:

God so loved us that he sent his only son (Jn. 3:16).

And since then, nothing has been the same!

Love changes everything. Love is the most powerful, the most energizing, the
most transforming force in the world.

Teilhard de Chardin reminded us that "someday after mastering the winds,
the waves, the tides and gravity, we shall harness for God the energies of love,
and then for a second time in the history of the world, we will have discovered fire."

Our memories, like sparks of that fire, are reservoirs of the power of the love
that we have experienced.

To recall the first moment of realizing that you were loved by a particular
person is to be present again at that moment in time.

It is to be in touch again with the astonishment that he/she would love **you**.
That other person appeared to be so self assured, so superior. Why would he/she
even take notice of you, much less be attracted or care?

Out of the astonishment came the questions.

Did you ask yourself: what is this going to mean for me?

Did you say, "It is only a passing thing, a moment's diversion"?

Did you, perhaps, turn away with, "No thank you, I'm busy"?

Somehow the love offered was too much to resist for long. When did you make the first response leading to the surrender which released and changed everything?

Love transforms, but not only in its initial surge of excitement, enjoyment and new energy. It continues through the years to draw one toward wholeness, that is, to becoming all that one is meant to be — a loved and loving person.

The miracle is when it continues, when love has proved not to be a passing phase. Is anything so amazing as the fidelity of another loving us, that is, continuing to put self and interests aside for us?

If love between two people can have such an effect, the love that God extends to us in Jesus is even more astonishing, incomprehensible. The love toward which our human loving points is that which St. Paul describes as ". . . the love of God . . . poured into our hearts by the Holy Spirit which has been given us" (Rm. 5:5).

However transforming and life giving a human love may be it is transcended by God's love for us.

That love remains a mystery. To speak of God's love as greater or better is too simplistic. God is not a bigger or better parent / lover / friend. Yet it is within our own human experience that we can intuit the incomprehensible love of God. In our human loving, we are like blind people, tracing with tentative fingers the unseen features of the face of God.

Within our fragile efforts to be consistent and faithful in our loving of each other, we catch a glimpse of the uniquely enduring quality of God's faithful love . . . a love made human for us in Jesus.

Through the death / resurrection of Jesus the Spirit is released, and we are plunged into a fullness of a relationship with God and with each other.

The death of Jesus is not, as has been commonly assumed by many, the result of an offended God punishing a "stand-in" for sinful humanity.

We need to approach the Crucified, and see how much we are loved, to see there the kind of love that would prompt our own willingness to give our life for someone we love. And we can, even within the limitations of human loving, image ourselves dying for our spouse, children, friends. What seems impossible is to die for someone else, unknown, unloved. And what seems even more impossible, is that someone would do that for **me**.

This is precisely what Paul says God has done for us in Jesus.

Jesus' death was the ultimate act of love for us. There is nothing more he could have done to show his love. And he did it voluntarily.

The love that shaped his death is the love that heals us, restores us, transforms us. That love continues to be poured out for us through the presence of Jesus risen — glorious, yet still bearing the wounds of his passion. He heals us in calling us to our own goodness, and continues to do so.

Through his death / resurrection, we are summoned into the presence of the Risen Jesus. We need only to believe and to surrender to that love, to say yes.

Though we continue to carry our woundedness, the wonder and beauty of our faith is that in the surrender the spirit of the Resurrection is released in and through us.

And we, as Christians — as Christ-bearers — so live as to share with the world the love of our God as we daily lay down our own lives for each other.

The Spirit of God's love, a spirit of trust that can empower us to live in joyful hope, has been poured into our hearts.

SUGGESTED APPROACH TO PRAYER: BEFORE THE CRUCIFIED

+ Daily prayer pattern, pages 1 and 2.
>   I quiet myself and relax in the presence of God.
>   I declare my dependency on God.
+ Grace:
>   I ask for the grace to experience the great love God has offered to me in and through Jesus.
+ Method: Meditation, page 2.
>   I reread the passage slowly, letting the words wash over me, savoring those that particularly attract me.
>   I go before the Crucified. I see Jesus hanging there, arms outstretched. I speak to him as friend to friend. I hear him speak to me of his love for me,

in creating me, in being willing to die for me. I let the questions fill my heart:

How have I through my life responded to the love of Christ?

How am I responding now?

To what does his love call me?

+ Closing: I pray the Our Father

+ Review of Prayer:

I write in my journal any responses I have had to the questions as well as any feelings I have experienced during this prayer period.

the choice
for
darkness

2 PETER 2:1-22

As there were false prophets in the past history of our people,
so you too will have your false teachers, who will insinuate
their own disruptive views and disown the Master who pur-
chased their freedom. They will destroy themselves very quickly;
but there will be many who copy their shameful behavior
and the Way of Truth will be brought into disrepute on their
account. They will eagerly try to buy you for themselves with
insidious speeches, but for them the Condemnation, pronounced
so long ago, is at its work already, and Destruction is not
asleep. When angels sinned, God did not spare them; he sent
them down to the underworld and consigned them to the dark
underground caves to be held there till the day of Judgment.
Nor did he spare the world in ancient times: it was only Noah
he saved, the preacher of righteousness, along with seven others,
when he sent the Flood over a disobedient world. The cities of
Sodom and Gomorrah, these too he condemned and reduced to
ashes; he destroyed them completely, as a warning to anybody
lacking reverence in the future; he rescued Lot, however, a holy
man who had been sickened by the shameless way in which
these vile people behaved — for that holy man, living among
them, was outraged in his good soul by the crimes that he saw
and heard of every day. These are all examples of how the Lord
can rescue the good from the ordeal, and hold the wicked for
their punishment until the day of Judgment, especially those
who are governed by their corrupt bodily desires and have no
respect for authority.

Such self-willed people with no reverence are not afraid of
offending against the glorious ones, but the angels in their
greater strength and power make no complaint or accusation

against them in front of the Lord. All the same, these people who only insult anything that they do not understand are not reasoning beings, but simply animals born to be caught and killed, and they will quite certainly destroy themselves by their own work of destruction, and get their reward of evil for the evil that they do. They are unsightly blots on your society: [persons] whose only object is dissipation all day long, and they amuse themselves deceiving you even when they are your guests at a meal; with their eyes always looking for adultery, [people] with an infinite capacity for sinning, they will seduce any soul which is at all unstable. Greed is the one lesson their minds have learned. They are under a curse. They have left the right path and wandered off to follow the path of Balaam, son of Beor, who thought he could profit best by sinning, until he was called to order for his faults. The dumb donkey put a stop to that prophet's madness when it talked like a [human being]. People like this are dried-up rivers, fogs swirling in the wind, and the dark underworld is the place reserved for them. With their high-flown talk, which is all hollow, they tempt back the ones who have only just escaped from paganism, playing on their bodily desires with debaucheries. They may promise freedom but they themselves are slaves, slaves to corruption; because if anyone lets himself be dominated by anything, then he is a slave to it; and anyone who has escaped the pollution of the world once by coming to know our Lord and savior Jesus Christ, and who then allows himself to be entangled by it a second time and mastered, will end up in worse state then he began in. It would even have been better for [that person] never to have learned the way of holiness, than to know it and afterward desert the holy rule that was entrusted to him. What he has done is exactly as the proverb rightly says: "The dog goes back to his own vomit" and: When the sow has been washed, it wallows in the mud.

COMMENTARY:

This passage is one of many instances throughout scripture giving evidence of a tradition that, even before the creation of the earth, a spirit of evil had been unleashed in defiance of God.

In our Judeo-Christian tradition this inherent idea was personified in the story of the fall of the angels.

In the story, the angels were the first and most magnificent of all of God's creations. They were under the rule and leadership of Lucifer whose name meant "light bearer." The angels were free, pure spirits and had been given the gift of free will.

God tested this freedom with an ultimate choice. Some of the angels failed, and they were cast into darkness. Lucifer — light-bearer — henceforth became known as the Prince of Darkness.

We do not know exactly what the test was. St. Thomas suggests that it was one of pride, the motive of which was excellence. Created in the purity of grace, the angels were not prone to sin. Their rejection of God was an act of free choice.

Some would suggest that they were shown a preview of God becoming human in the infant Jesus and were asked to worship him. Their sin would, then, have been one of refusal to submit to the seeming inferiority of Jesus.

With that one act, the darkness enveloped them.

The story of the fall of the angels provides us with an archetype, that is, a collective primal representation in which we can grasp the deep rootedness of our own cosmic sin situation.

It is not enough for us to realize the pervasive darkness that over-shadows our nuclear/technological age. We need to go beyond that, to recognize that "sinfulness reaches down into the immense abyss of a sin occurring in a pure spirit." (59, p. 47). There is no immunity to sin.

The story is like a mirror in which, as we view the fall of the angels, we see reflected our own foolish, rebellious choices — not once as for the angels, but many times.

In the second letter of Peter, the reference to the fall of the angels is made within the description of the subversive forces faced by the early Church. False

22

teachers, seductive leaders, and politically corrupt influential people were making inroads among the members of the young Christian community. The corrupt leaders were motivated by greed and offered false promises of social freedom.

Peter warns the people of impending punishment, using examples from the past. He presents as the ideal Noah and Lot who, while living in the midst of evil, stood firm and did not conform.

When the angels sinned, God did not spare them.

Yet God is merciful to his people.

SUGGESTED APPROACH TO PRAYER: INTO A MIRROR

+ Daily prayer pattern, pages 1 and 2.
    I quiet myself and relax in the presence of God.
    I declare my dependency on God.
+ Grace:
    I ask for the grace of feeling shame and confusion as I reflect on the effect of one sin of the angels, especially when I consider my own many selfish choices. (cf. p.x)
+ Method: I prayerfully reread the commentary.
    I image myself looking into a mirror of imagination and memory. I will let the story of the fall of the angels unfold before me. In mind and heart, I mull over the incredibility of the single decision and rebellious action of the angels and its effects. I look at my own many choices and acts which have been a turning away from God's love.
+ Closing:
    I image Christ crucified. I speak to him, in my own words, of this great mystery. Through one sin of rejecting God's love, the angels were condemned. I, who have repeatedly rejected his love through sin, am allowed to continue to live and am given many "second chances." I close my prayer with an Our Father.
+ Review of Prayer:
    I write in my journal any feelings, experiences or insights that have surfaced during this prayer period.

GENESIS 3:1-7

> *The serpent was the most subtle of all the wild beasts that*
> *Yahweh God had made. It asked the woman, "Did God really*
> *say you were not to eat from any of the trees in the garden?"*
> *The woman answered the serpent, "We may eat the fruit of the*
> *trees in the garden. But of the fruit of the tree in the middle of*
> *the garden God said, 'You must not eat it, nor touch it, under*
> *pain of death.' " Then the serpent said to the woman, "No! You*
> *will not die! God knows in fact that on the day you eat it your*
> *eyes will be opened and you will be like gods, knowing good*
> *and evil." The woman saw that the tree was good to eat and*
> *pleasing to the eye, and that it was desirable for the knowledge*
> *that it could give. So she took some of its fruit and ate it. She*
> *gave some also to her husband who was with her, and he ate*
> *it. Then the eyes of both of them were opened and they realized*
> *they were naked. So they sewed fig leaves together to make*
> *themseves loincloths.*

COMMENTARY:

"Something went wrong in the human family to which I belong" (72, p. 79).

What went wrong is depicted for us in the story of Adam and Eve as it is found in Genesis 3:1-7. Like the actors in a play, Adam, Eve and the serpent enter upon the stage. As we watch, listen and are drawn into the story, we are confronted with our own situation. It is not that we journey backward into time, but that we look within the depth of ourselves and see there our collective solidarity with the human family.

The story is part of our heritage, enriched with the symbols, the poetry and the folk tales of its telling over four thousand years.

The stage is set in the garden of Eden, in primitive blessedness. Adam and Eve dwell there within an innocent state of freedom. All their needs are met and

24

they are in intimate friendship with God who walks companionably with them each evening.

The one condition that God has given them is that they not eat of the tree of good and evil. The prohibition regarding this tree represents the danger of going beyond the bounds of their creaturehood, beyond who God intended them to be.

God did not place upon them this condition because he was jealous or threatened that they might compete with Him. Rather, God knew that within each individual there exists a great drive for the fullness of mental and physical powers.

God knew that the fullness could come only by the acceptance of their own creaturehood and in their surrendering to his love. So powerful is the drive toward a fullness of self that it holds the potential threat of propelling the human creature into a denial of the truer self, and thereby denying God.

The prohibition was an expression of and protection for the law within the human heart which holds in balance the tension of creature and Creator.

The common interpretation of the tree in terms of pleasure, possessions and power are all contained within this pursuit of self, in the drive toward completeness.

The ultimate choice is self or God.

Enter the serpent! The tempting question arises through creation itself in the form of the serpent, seen for centuries as a symbol of evil. For the Hebrew people, the serpent personified the dark powers of healing, of sorcery and of limitless power (8, p. 45).

Eve and Adam were faced with the choice.

So the woman "took some of its fruit and ate it. She gave some also to her husband . . . and he ate it. Then the eyes of both of them were opened. . . ."

The world they saw before them was not the world they had envisioned. It was, instead, a world of darkness.

They attempted to hide from the presence of God. But in the cool of the evening, he inquired, "Where are you?"

They were filled with fear and shame. They blamed each other and the serpent.

The fall of the angels, the first of God's creations, had been reenacted in the first of human creatures.

In the last scene of this act, Adam and Eve are expelled from the garden of their innocence.

SUGGESTED APPROACH TO PRAYER:

+ Daily prayer pattern, pages 1 and 2.
  I quiet myself and relax in the presence of God.
  I declare my dependency on God.
+ Grace:
  I ask for the grace of feeling shame and confusion as I reflect on the effects of the one sin of Adam and Eve and I consider my own many selfish and sinful choices.
+ Method: Contemplation, page 3.
  I place myself in the garden with Adam and Eve. In imagination I will enjoy the beauty and fragrance of the flowers, the sounds of the water, and the presence of the animals. I accompany Adam and Eve as they walk and talk with God. I continue to image the story in detail and follow it through to its completion: the entrance of the serpent, the disobedience of Adam and Eve, and the consequences.
+ Closing:
  I image Christ crucified. I speak in my own words of how for one sin the angels were doomed; for one sin Adam and Eve were expelled from the garden. And I, who have so frequently chosen self in favor of God and yet have been spared, how is it that I am not in hell? I close my prayer with an Our Father.
+ Review of Prayer:
  I write in my journal any interior feelings, experiences or insights that have surfaced during this prayer period.

ROMANS 5:12-21

Well, then, sin entered the world through one man, and through sin death, and thus death has spread through the whole human race because everyone has sinned. Sin existed in the world long before the Law was given. There was no law and so no one could be accused of the sin of "lawbreaking," yet death reigned over all from Adam to Moses, even though their sin, unlike that of Adam, was not a matter of breaking a law.

Adam prefigured the One to come, but the gift itself considerably outweighed the fall. If it is certain that through one man's fall so many died, it is even more certain that divine grace, coming through the one man, Jesus Christ, came to so many as an abundant free gift. The results of the gift also outweigh the results of one man's sin: for after one single fall came judgment with a verdict of condemnation, now after many falls comes grace with its verdict of acquittal. If it is certain that death reigned over everyone as the consequence of one man's fall, it is even more certain that one man, Jesus Christ, will cause everyone to reign in life who receives the free gift that he does not deserve, of being made righteous. Again, as one man's fall brought condemnation on everyone, so the good act of one [person] brings everyone life and makes them justified. As by one [person's] disobedience many were made sinners, so by one [person's] obedience many will be made righteous. When law came, it was to multiply the opportunities of falling, but however great the number of sins committed, grace was even greater; and so, just as sin reigned wherever there was death, so grace will reign to bring eternal life thanks to the righteousness that comes through Jesus Christ our Lord.

27

COMMENTARY:

Adam sinned.

One person, one sin: darkness and pain followed.

Darkness and sin encircled the earth; no one has escaped its pervading tentacles. It spread into entire families, into the very earth itself. Through one act, sin entered the world and began to trace its path through history. No person, no social structure, sector, or institution has escaped its viral presence.

Each of us, in this historical, collective dimension, sees ourself in Adam and Eve and the penance of this original sin is visited on each of us. The past did not occur apart from our present reality. Our present reality is held within our past.

In every act of sin that is committed the original sin of Adam and Eve is ratified (59, p. 49).

Darkness precipitates darkness in . . .

— the breakdown of family with Cain and Abel (Gen 4:1-16) then and now;
— the breakdown of communication at Babel (Gen 11:1-9) . . . then and now;
— the flood of wickedness (Gen 6:5ff), then . . . and now.

Into this darkness, Jesus comes.

"Just as all die in Adam, so all will be brought to life in Christ . . ." (I Cor 15:22).

Through a total surrender to God, Jesus reversed the choice of Adam. In Jesus, Adam's choice has been annulled.

Paul parallels Adam and Christ. It is not, however, as if they are equal counter forces. "Where death does abound, there does life **more** abound" (Rm 5:21 paraphrase).

Good far outweighs evil and in Jesus the death and destruction of sin is overturned.

SUGGESTED APPROACH TO PRAYER:

+ Daily prayer pattern, pages 1 and 2.
    I quiet myself and relax in the presence of God.
    I declare my dependency on God.

28

+ Grace:

I ask for the grace of feeling shame and confusion as I consider the effects of sin.

+ Method:

I carefully consider the passage of Paul and the commentary, with an awareness of the widespread destructiveness of sin in our world. I consider how, if one act of sin was such a strong catalyst for so much evil in the world, what about my own many sins? *Or, focus on Christ' greater gift.*

+ Closing:

I go before the Crucified and reflect about this mystery of sin and speak to Christ of whatever surfaces in my mind and heart. I close my prayer with the Our Father.

+ Review of Prayer:

I write in my journal any feelings, experiences or insights that have come to my awareness during this prayer period.

ST. LUKE 16:19-31

There was a rich man who used to dress in purple and fine linen and feast magnificently every day. And at his gate there lay a poor man called Lazarus, covered with sores, who longed to fill himself with the scraps that fell from the rich man's table. Dogs even came and licked his sores. Now the poor man died and was carried away by the angels to the bosom of Abraham. The rich man also died and was buried.

In his torment in Hades he looked up and saw Abraham a long way off with Lazarus in his bosom. So he cried out, "Father Abraham, pity me and send Lazarus to dip the tip of his finger in water and cool my tongue, for I am in agony in these flames." "My son," Abraham replied, "remember that during your life good things came your way, just as bad things came the way of Lazarus. Now he is being comforted here while you are in agony. But that is not all: between us and you a great gulf has been fixed to stop anyone if he wanted to, crossing from our side to yours, and to stop any crossing from your side to ours."

The rich man replied, "Father, I beg you then to send Lazarus to my father's house, since I have five brothers, to give them warning so that they do not come to this place of torment too." "They have Moses and the prophets," said Abraham, "let them listen to them." "Ah no, father Abraham," said the rich man, "but if someone comes to them from the dead, they will repent." Then Abraham said to him, "If they will not listen either to Moses or to the prophets, they will not be convinced even if someone should rise from the dead."

COMMENTARY:

The sin of the rich man was not that he was rich.

But he was rich!

He was rich materially; he dressed in fine linen and royal purple, the dye of which was obtained from exotic shellfish available only to the very wealthy. The color itself was a status symbol.

Every day was a gourmet feast! In a country where meat was scarce, he ate it daily.

He was rich, also, by privilege and status.

As a Sadducee, he was a member of the established religion. While allowing him the exercise of power and influence, membership in this group carried with it the assumption that he was above reproach, that is, righteous.

The rich man who, as a Sadducee, did not believe in life after death, ironically discovers himself in acute suffering cut off from life and condemned to eternal loss.

He looks over the abyss that separates the damned from those who have been delivered into the presence of God. There he sees Lazarus welcomed and enfolded in the love of the God of Abraham.

For the first time, the rich man recognizes and calls Lazarus by name. Yet, even in these circumstances, the rich man treats Lazarus as his servant.

The sin of the rich man was not the fact of his wealth or status. It was not that he was openly or deliberately cruel. He had not, after all, had Lazarus removed from his gate. He didn't necessarily forbid him the scraps.

He simply did not notice him, and that was his sin!

Lazarus had become for the rich man an inevitable part of the social structure, always present, always unseen.

As an ancient folk tale that Luke uses to carry forward his theme of the exaltation of the lowly and the "putting down" of the mighty (Lk 1:52), this parable is more than a simple reversal of external circumstances. It is more than a story illustrating the reward of poverty and the punishment of the wealthy. It is a warning!

The story is a warning to those who claim to be believers, hearing God's word in scripture and worship, and who do not bring their daily lives into accord with God's word.

It was part of Hebrew belief that land owners were tenants of Yahweh (Lev. 25:23) who paid "taxes" through alms to the poor who were Yahweh's representatives.

The rich man's blind indifference to Lazarus was a rejection, not only of God's word, but a rejection of God.

This was the sin of the rich man.

For the rich man, for his brothers and for us, there are two failures which belong together: "Where the mind is closed to the revelation of God, the heart is closed to the demands of compassion" (16, 192).

SUGGESTED APPROACH TO PRAYER:

+ Daily prayer pattern, pages 1 and 2.
   I quiet myself and relax in the presence of God.
   I declare my dependency on God.
+ Grace:
   I ask for the grace of feeling shame and confusion as I consider the effects of sin, and of amazement before the goodness and mercy of God in preserving me from hell.
+ Method: Contemplation, page 3.
   I assume the role of the rich man and image myself wearing beautiful robes and feasting sumptuously. I see myself being unaware of suffering around me. I image, in great detail, myself being in hell. I see my shock, confusion and futile cry for release. I am aware of the images and conversations that are occurring.
+ Closing:
   I go before the Crucified and, considering my own sinfulness, my own unawareness, I ask, "Why have I been preserved from the ultimate effect of my sinfulness?" I close my prayer with an Our Father.
+ Review of Prayer:
   I write in my journal any feelings, experiences or insights that have surfaced during this prayer period.

SUGGESTED APPROACH TO PRAYER:

+ Daily prayer pattern, pages 1 and 2.
    I quiet myself and relax in the presence of God.
    I declare my dependency on God.
+ Grace:
    I ask for the grace of feeling deep confusion and sorrow as I consider
the effects of even one sin.
+ Method: It will be particularly helpful to read "Repetition" on page 6.
    In preparation I review my prayer by reading my journal of the past
week. I select for my repetition the period of prayer in which I was deeply
moved, either by joy or sadness. I proceed in the manner I did originally,
focusing on the scene, word, or feeling that was previously significant.
+ Review of Prayer:
    I write in my journal any feelings, experiences or insights that have
come to my awareness during this prayer period.

the
Consequences
of
sin

EZEKIEL 16:1-22; 59-63

The word of Yahweh was addressed to me as follows, "Son of man, confront Jerusalem with her filthy crimes. Say, 'The Lord Yahweh says this: By origin and birth you belong to the land of Canaan. Your father was an Amorite and your mother a Hittite. At birth, the very day you were born, there was no one to cut your navel string, or wash you in cleansing water, or rub you with salt, or wrap you in napkins. No one leaned kindly over you to do anything like that for you. You were exposed in the open fields; you were as unloved as that on the day you were born.

I saw you struggling in your blood as I was passing, and I said to you as you lay in your blood: Live, and grow like the grass of the fields. You developed, you grew, you reached marriageable age. Your breasts and your hair both grew, but you were quite naked. Then I saw you as I was passing. Your time had come, the time for love. I spread part of my cloak over you and covered your nakedness; I bound myself by oath, I made a covenant with you — it is the Lord Yahweh who speaks — and you became mine. I bathed you in water, I washed the blood off you, I anointed you with oil. I gave you embroidered dresses, fine leather shoes, a linen headband and a cloak of silk. I loaded you with jewels, gave you bracelets for your wrists and a necklace for your throat. . . . You were loaded with gold and silver, and dressed in fine linen and embroidered silks. Your food was the finest flour, honey and oil. You grew more and more beautiful; and you rose to be queen. The fame of your beauty spread through the nations, since it was perfect, because I had clothed you with my own splendor — it is the Lord Yahweh who speaks.

36

You have become infatuated with your own beauty; you have used your fame to make yourself a prostitute; you have offered your services to all comers . . . You have taken your clothes to brighten your high places and there you have played the whore . . . You have taken my presents of gold and silver jewelry and made yourself human images to use in your whorings. You have taken your embroidered clothes and put them on the images, and the oil and incense which are rightly mine you have offered to them. The bread I gave you, the finest flour, oil and honey with which I used to feed you, you have now offered to them as an appeasing fragrance.

You have even — it is the Lord Yahweh who speaks — taken the sons and daughters you bore me and sacrificed them as food to the images. Was it not enough for you just to be a whore? You have slaughtered my children and handed them over as a burnt offering to them, and in all your filthy practices and your whorings you have never remembered your youth or the time when you were quite naked and struggling in your own blood.
. . . .

For the Lord Yahweh says this: I will treat you as you deserve, you who have despised your oath even to the extent of breaking a covenant, but I will remember the covenant that I made with you when you were a girl, and I will conclude a covenant with you that shall last forever. And you for your part will remember your past behavior and be covered with shame when I take your elder and younger sisters and make them your daughters, although this was not included in this covenant. I am going to renew my covenant with you; and you will learn that I am Yahweh, and so remember and be covered with shame, and in your confusion be reduced to silence, when I have pardoned you for all that you have done — it is the Lord Yahweh who speaks."

COMMENTARY:

Ezekiel's long and dramatic oracle expresses his grief and abhorrence of sin in the light of God's goodness. Not generally found in scripture, the lurid images and strong language may be offensive on first reading.

This oracle is a prophetic warning. It takes the form of a story about the life of an abandoned child, who after having been found and cared for, rejected love and adopted a life of prostitution.

Though the typical exposure folk tale of his time focused on the foundling as a hero, Ezekiel focused his story on the faithfulness of God in the face of the unfaithfulness of the foundling. While the "foundling as hero" is always very appealing, Ezekiel uses the story like a two-edged sword to cut through and expose the reality and treachery of sin.

The story is an allegory of the history of the chosen people and their relationship with God. A parallelism is drawn between the life of the prostitute and the history of the Israelite people.

Like the beginings of the life of the foundling, Israel's beginnings, too, were in the wilderness of Egypt. In God's "passing," Israel, like the child, grew in stature and beauty.

At the point of readiness, God claimed the young woman as his own. Israel, too, was chosen, and the relationship with God was like that of a marriage covenant.

Not unlike the prostitute's rejection of love, Israel's history is a recital of idolatry and infidelity. The chosen people made alliances with foreign kings, adopting their cultic worship of foreign gods. They even went so far as to practice human sacrifice.

As the passage is read, one is overwhelmed with the sense of the malignant destructive character of sin. Self-perpetuating and parasitical, sin releases an alienating force of such strength that it isolates us from ourselves and consequently from God.

This is the anguish of Ezekiel as he ponders Israel's history of infidelity.

Ezekiel's main thrust is to move the prostitute towards a sense of shame and confusion. He calls on her to remember God's goodness to her, and how faithful God had always been.

38

Only in the memory of God's overwhelming love for her will she plumb the depths of her shame, be filled with sorrow for her sin and be reconciled.

For the prostitute, for Israel, and for us, "the shame and disgrace over the past bespeaks the new impressionable, contrite heart that will animate the future . . ." (33, p. 306).

SUGGESTED APPROACH TO PRAYER:

+ Daily prayer pattern, pages 1 and 2.
> I quiet myself and relax in the presence of God.
> I declare my dependency on God.

+ Grace: I ask for the grace of sorrow for sin.

+ Method:
> I will read the passage and the commentary carefully. As the story and its meaning become clear, I will be aware of my feelings, e.g., my repulsions, anxieties. I will ask myself the following questions:
>> Can I, in any way, identify with the foundling — abandoned and uncared for?
>> Can I identify with the prostitute?
>> What questions surface within me?

+ Closing:
> I will speak with Christ on the cross. I will share with him whatever I have experienced through Ezekiel's passage. I close my prayer with an Our Father.

+ Review of Prayer:
> I write in my journal my responses to the questions posed above.

Reread Ezekiel 16:1-22; 59-63 (cf. pp. 36 and 37).

COMMENTARY:

In a time when only a few people knew how to read, the early Israelites were almost totally dependent on memory. Repeatedly in the Old Testament, we find them being instructed to "remember."

"Remember the sabbath day and keep it holy" (Ex 20:8).

"Remember the marvels he has done. . . . Remember his covenant forever . . ." (Ps. 105:5, 8).

The first five books of the Bible, called the Torah — Law — contain the early history and stories, the memory of the Hebrew people.

Although there were, in the Torah, many specific requirements with which the people were to regulate their lives, the essential, underlying **law** was that the people were never to forget God's goodness to them.

They were to recall in memory all the events and circumstances of their common history, in which Yahweh revealed his love and choice. They were to celebrate his presence — past, present and future.

At the heart of their worship was the remembrance of God's deed, their affirmation of his presence among them, and their trust in the new thing he would create among them.

"Now I am revealing new things to you, things hidden and unknown to you, created just now, this very moment . . ." (Is 48:6; see also Rev. 21:5).

Memory endowed the Hebrew people, and endows us, with a sense of rootedness, identity and direction.

To prayerfully remember is to cooperate with God in the re-membering of ourselves. It is to actively engage with the Spirit in uniting those fragmented areas of ourselves which have been split off and alienated through sin.

As we recall a particular event or circumstance in which we experienced God's love sustaining and directing us, two things occur: there is a deepening awareness of his faithfulness and, in the recalling, we open ourselves, mysteriously, to receive again the grace of that event, this time in greater measure with a deeper level of healing and integration.

So, "remember and be covered with shame" (Ez. 16:63).

SUGGESTED APPROACH TO PRAYER:

+ Daily prayer pattern, pages 1 and 2.
>   I quiet myself and relax in the presence of God.
>   I declare my dependency on God.
+ Grace: I ask for the gift of sorrow for sin.
+ Method:
>   I walk through my life, remembering places I loved, and events, activities, work, significant people. I recall God's eruptions of love, and how I have exploited, misused or rejected that love:

GOD'S LOVE   MY REJECTION

As a child

As an adolescent

Years: 20-30

Years: 30-40

Years: 40-50

Years: 50 and over

You may find it helpful to write this exercise in your journal.

41

+ Closing:

I see Christ on the cross. I thank him for his compassion toward me throughout my life. I thank him that he has sustained me to this point. I close with an Our Father.

+ Review of Prayer:

I write in my journal any new awareness that came to me during this prayer exercise.

Reread Ezekiel 16:1-22; 59-63 (cf. pp. 36 and 37).

COMMENTARY:

Reread the passage and review whatever journaling you have done in the past two days of prayer.

SUGGESTED APPROACH TO PRAYER:

+ Daily prayer pattern, pages 1 and 2.
    I quiet myself and relax in the presence of God.
    I declare my dependency on God.
+ Grace: I ask for shame and confusion because of my sinfulness.
+ Method:
    I return to the prayer of the previous day, my own history of grace and sin, of God's love and my own rejection. As I review sin history, I focus my attention on whichever particular sin event God allows to surface most prominently. I prayerfully place myself in the situation of that event. I recall in detail all the specific aspects . . . the place, the people, the words, thoughts and feelings.
        I consider the consequences of this sin:
        What has occurred as a result?
        How has it been destructive of relationships?
        How has it limited possibilities for myself and others?
        What suffering has come about through my sin? Who has wept?
        How has it reinforced and contributed to the evil that I see in the world?
+ Closing:
    I see Christ on the cross. I speak to him from the depths of my awareness. I thank him for not deserting me in my times of sin and brokenness.
+ Review of Prayer:
    I write in my journal my responses to the questions posed above.

2 SAMUEL 11:1-21, 27; 12:1, 7-10, 13-25

At the turn of the year, the time when kings go campaigning, David sent Joab and with him his own guards and the whole of Israel. They massacred the Ammonites and laid siege to Rabbah. David however remained in Jerusalem.

It happened toward evening when David had risen from his couch and was strolling on the palace roof, that he saw from the roof a woman bathing; the woman was very beautiful. David made inquiries about this woman and was told, "Why, that is Bathsheba, Eliam's daughter, the wife of Uriah the Hittite." Then David sent messengers and had her brought. She came to him and he slept with her; now she had just purified herself from her courses. She then went home again. The woman conceived and sent word to David, "I am with child."

Then David sent Joab a message, "Send me Uriah, the Hittite," whereupon Joab sent Uriah to David. When Uriah came into his presence, David asked after Joab and the army and how the war was going. David then said to Uriah, "Go down to your house and enjoy yourself." Uriah left the palace, and was followed by a present from the king's table. Uriah however slept by the palace door with his master's bodyguard and did not go down to his house.

This was reported to David; "Uriah," they said, "did not go down to his house." So David asked Uriah, "Have you not just arrived from a journey? Why do you not go to your home?" But Uriah answered, "Are not the ark and the men of Israel and Judah lodged in tents; and my master Joab and the bodyguard of my lord, are they not in the open fields?

Am I to go to my house, then, and eat and drink and sleep with my wife? As Yahweh lives, and as you yourself live, I will do no such thing!" Then David said to Uriah, "Stay on here today; tomorrow I will send you back." So Uriah stayed that day in Jerusalem. The next day David invited him to eat and drink in his presence and made him drunk. In the evening Uriah went out and lay on his couch with his master's bodyguard, but he did not go down to his house.

Next morning David wrote a letter to Joab and sent it by Uriah. In the letter he wrote, "Station Uriah in the thick of the fight and then fall back behind him so that he may be struck down and die." Joab, then besieging the town, posted Uriah in a place where he knew there were fierce fighters. The men of the town sallied out and engaged Joab; the army suffered casualties, including some of David's bodyguard; and Uriah the Hittite was killed too.

Joab sent David a full account of the battle. To the messenger he gave this order: "When you have finished telling the king all the details of the battle, the king's anger may be provoked; he may say, 'Why did you go so near the town to fight? Did you not know they would shoot from the ramparts? Who killed Abimelech son of Jerubbaal? Was it not a woman who dropped a millstone on him from the ramparts, causing his death at Thebez? Why did you go so near the ramparts?' If so, you are to say, 'Your servant Uriah the Hittite has been killed too.'" . . . When the period of mourning was over, David sent to have her brought to his house; she became his wife and bore him a son. But what David had done displeased Yahweh.

Yahweh sent Nathan the prophet to David. He came to him and said, "You are the man. Yahweh the God of Israel says this, 'I anointed you king over Israel; I delivered you from the hands

45

of Saul; I gave your master's house to you, his wives into your arms; I gave you the House of Israel and of Judah; and if this were not enough, I would add as much again for you. Why have you shown contempt for Yahweh, doing what displeases him? You have struck down Uriah the Hittite with the sword, taken his wife for your own, and killed him with the sword of the Ammonites. So now the sword will never be far from your House, since you have shown contempt for me and taken the wife of Uriah the Hittite to be your wife. . . .

David said to Nathan, "I have sinned against Yahweh." Then Nathan said to David, "Yahweh, for his part, forgives your sin; you are not to die. Yet because you have outraged Yahweh by doing this, the child that is born to you is to die." Then Nathan went home.

Yahweh struck the child that Uriah's wife had borne to David, and it fell gravely ill. David pleaded with Yahweh for the child; he kept a strict fast and went home and spent the night on the bare ground, covered with sacking. The officials of his household came and stood around him to get him to rise from the ground, but he refused, nor would he take food with them. On the seventh day the child died. David's officers were afraid to tell him the child was dead. "Even when the child was alive," they thought, "we reasoned with him and he would not listen to us. How can we tell him the child is dead? He will do something desperate." David, however, noticed that his officers were whispering among themselves, and realized the child was dead. "Is the child dead?" he asked the officers. They answered, "He is dead."

David got up from the ground, bathed and anointed himself and put on fresh clothes. Then he went into the sanctuary of Yahweh and prostrated himself. On returning to his house he asked for food to be set before him, and ate. His officers said,

"Why are you acting like this? When the child was alive, you fasted and wept; now the child is dead, you get up and take food." "When the child was alive," he answered, "I fasted and wept because I kept thinking, 'Who knows? Perhaps Yahweh will take pity on me and the child will live.' But now he is dead, why should I fast? Can I bring him back again? I shall go to him, but he cannot come back to me."

David consoled his wife Bathsheba. He went to her and slept with her. She conceived and gave birth to a son whom she named Solomon. Yahweh loved him and made this known through the prophet Nathan who named him Jedidiah in accordance with the word of Yahweh.

COMMENTARY:

"You are the one."

The key image in this passage is the hard eyes, the jarring voice and the pointing finger of Nathan as he confronts David in his sinfulness.

"You are the one."

Nathan was addressing David, king of Israel and Judah. This was David, artistic, full of charm, a poet, a musician, a military hero. David was everything any one could ever aspire to be. God's hand had shaped the events of his life and had led him from victory to victory.

As the king of northern Israel and southern Judah, David wore a double crown. By the sheer force of his dynamic personality David welded of the two desperate entities, one nation, and he established Jerusalem as the site of his capital. He was, in effect, "the darling of Jerusalem."

In addition, God had bestowed on David yet another, more enduring blessing. God promised David that the future of Israel's deepest hope would be secured in David's descendants (2 Sm 7:13).

For his part, David had been exemplary. In the first half of his life he had been faithful to the unfolding of God's plan in the events that were shaping his destiny.

Yet, he sinned. At the pinnacle of his success, when life held the most promise, David was unfaithful. Even the king, even David, was not immune to sin!

Whereas the first book of Chronicles gives us an idealized picture of David, the author of the Second Book of Samuel shows us the paradox in David — the shadows as well as the light.

The confrontation of David by Nathan represents the moment in which David was forced to face that shadow, his sin.

Nathan's words pierced through the egotistical facade and self seeking to which David had succumbed.

What was challenged was not only the grievous sexual sin of passion with Bathsheba, but the deeper sin disposition from which that sin and those that followed were unleashed.

David had proceeded with cold deliberation to control and manipulate people and circumstances for his own selfish purposes.

Faced with his sin, David wept. He was unmasked. His carefully constructed defense system collapsed.

He who was the defender of the poor and arbiter of justice had himself stolen from the poor and made a mockery of the law of justice and charity.

He who was king experienced his own inner poverty and weakness. David was confronted with the painful reality that he had contributed to the power of evil.

The moment of awareness became for David the moment of confession and conversion.

David cried out, "I have sinned against Yahweh!"

David's experience of inner poverty became the stance of dependency before God. In the knowledge and acceptance of himself as sinner, David entered into a deeper reality.

In the moment of submitting himself to God, he rose from his weeping and resumed his task as king and guardian of Israel. He was never more human, more royal, more truly servant of God than at the moment of surrender.

The challenge of the prophet had become for David the call to life.

SUGGESTED APPROACH TO PRAYER:

+ Daily prayer pattern, pages 1 and 2.
   I quiet myself and relax in the presence of God.
   I declare my dependency on God.
+ Grace: I ask for intense sorrow for my sinfulness.
+ Method: Contemplation, as on page 3.
   I contemplate in detail the scene between David and Nathan. I assume the role of David. I experience Nathan's finger pointing at me. I listen to his stern voice as he accuses me. I am "the one." As I become aware of my own sinfulness, I let the weight of evil in my life be felt through my entire being.
+ Closing:
   I see Christ on the cross. I speak to him from the depths of my awareness. I close my prayer with the Our Father.
+ Review of Prayer:
   I write in my journal my feeling responses as I stand accused.

PSALM 130

> From the depths I call to you, Yahweh,
> Lord, listen to my cry for help!
> Listen compassionately
>   to my pleading!
>
> If you never overlooked our sins, Yahweh,
> Lord, could anyone survive?
> But you do forgive us:
>   and for that we revere you.
>
> I wait for Yahweh, my soul waits for him,
>   I rely on his promise,
>   my soul relies on the Lord
>   more than a watchman on the coming of dawn.
>
> Let Israel rely on Yahweh
>   as much as the watchman on the dawn!
> For it is with Yahweh that mercy is to be found,
> and a generous redemption;
> it is he who redeems Israel
>   from all their sins.

COMMENTARY:

"Out of the depths . . . **de profundis** . . . have I called to you, Lord."

Psalm 130 represents a profound cry for mercy and relief on the part of an individual who is experiencing desperation. He is feeling totally isolated and cut off from all love and meaning. He is literally begging God to listen.

Has there not been for each of us a moment, a night, when that same cry was wrung out of **our** being? A cry like this could arise from a number of situations, any of which would plunge one into an acute experience of pain or loss.

The experience from which the psalmist cries out is the anguish of being alienated from God and others through personal sinfulness.

The psalmist describes his anguish as coming from the "depths." The "depths" may refer to the poignancy of loss which is experienced by those who are in Sheol, that is, cast into the far-reaching shadowy after-death existence.

The depths may also hold the many-faceted symbol of chaotic waters. For the Hebrew people, the sea represented not only death, but birth and new creation (Gn. 1:2).

Though his suffering is extreme, the psalmist is not without hope. We hear him acknowledge God's forgiveness in spite of his many sins. He is counting on that forgiveness and admitting that no one really could deserve it. He is aware that the record of everyone is so contaminated that only God's pure gift of mercy could lift one from the depths of misery.

"But you do forgive us, and for that we revere you."

The hope is breathtaking. Not only does the psalmist count on God's forgiveness, but he knows that with the forgiveness also comes a "second favor."

Where there is forgiveness there follows a change of heart, there follows reverence.

Our English word, "reverence," has lost some of the fullness of the Hebrew word in its root meaning.

The original intention of reverence, as used in this passage, implies a fullness of religious experience such as would occur in **metanoia**, that is, in a total change of heart.

This reverence includes a dimension of fear. It is not an anxious flight-type fear as in the face of an impending danger. This is fear as awe or sense of wonder which is inspired by one to whom we are strongly attracted yet who is so far above us that our only authentic response is one of adoration.

The fear inspired by forgiveness is the harbinger, the messenger, that a new revelation of God has taken place. This revelation enables the repentant sinner to see God as he has never seen him before and to relate to Him in a new way.

An example of this "new way" of seeing and relating to God can be recalled in the experience of Moses and the Israelite people during their time in the desert. After having received the tablets inscribed with the law, Moses returned to the

51

people to find them engaged in the worship of false gods. Both God and Moses were outraged at the sin. Moses pleaded for his people.

In the moment of forgiveness, God gave a further revelation of Himself: Moses "called on the name of Yahweh. Yahweh passed before him and proclaimed, 'Yahweh, Yahweh, a God of tenderness and compassion, slow to anger, rich in kindness and faithfulness; for thousands he maintains his kindness, forgives faults, transgressions, sin; yet he lets nothing go unchecked, punishing the father's fault in the sons and in the grandsons to the third and fourth generation" (Ex. 34:6-7).

To be forgiven is to see God, and to be impelled to awe, to loving gratitude, to trust. And that is to worship.

In the psalm, the sinner is awaiting the fullness of forgiveness he knows will come. He turns to the community of Israel and instructs them, also, to wait.

Both he and Israel are experiencing the darkness of night, the absence of God. We need only to remember our own experience of waiting in the night, how we kept looking for the darkness to give way to the first hint of morning light. Even more, the psalmist awaits the dawn of God's forgiveness. Through that forgiveness he and the community will be restored and made whole in a new and renewed vision.

SUGGESTED APPROACH TO PRAYER:

+ Daily prayer pattern, pages 1 and 2.
   I quiet myself and relax in the presence of God.
   I declare my dependency on God.

+ Grace: I ask for a growing and intense sorrow for sin, even for the gift of tears.

+ Method: I pray this psalm out of the depths of my own sinfulness as I consider:

   • how my sin has alienated me from my self, has deprived me of my sense of self worth, and has been an obstacle to my becoming the unique person God intends me to be;

   • how the saints through their deliberate choices have become whole

52

and holy, while I through my deliberate sinful choices have fragmented and spiritually crippled myself;

- how, though I was created to be in close relationship with God, my Creator, and to be in harmony with and give praise with all creation, I have made choices to depend on myself alone and have, as a consequence, alienated myself from God, from others and from creation;
- how my physical and intellectual limitations and fragility is an experience of the effects of sin;
- how I have, through my sinfulness, contributed to the movement of evil in the world.

+ Closing: I go before Jesus crucified and speak to him of whatever comes to mind and heart.

+ Review of Prayer:

I write in my journal my growing sense of sorrow for my sinfulness.

JOB 42:1-6

> *This was the answer Job gave to Yahweh:*
> *I know that you are all-powerful:*
> > *what you conceive, you can perform.*
> *I am the man who obscured your designs*
> > *with my empty-headed words.*
> *I have been holding forth on matters I cannot understand,*
> > *on marvels beyond me and my knowledge.*
> *(Listen, I have more to say,*
> > *now it is my turn to ask questions and*
> > *yours to inform me.)*
> *I knew you then only by hearsay;*
> > *but now, having seen you with my own eyes,*
> *I retract all I have said,*
> > *and in dust and ashes I repent.*

COMMENTARY:

Job is Job and God is God. It is in this awareness that Job, at last, surrenders, and finds joy.

Job is Job and God is God.

This simple assertion expresses the core message not only of verses 1-6, but of the entire book of Job.

These verses are the climax and resolution of a long and tortuous faith struggle on the part of Job.

Job was a deeply religious man, influential and successful. He had a loving wife and family, was a large property owner, and had acquired wealth.

Satan challenged God by discrediting Job's faith. Satan made a wager with God that if Job were deprived of the comfort of his family, wealth and influence, his faith would crumble.

God agreed to the testing of Job's faith.

Gradually, Job was stripped of his family, his possessions and even his health.

Bewildered by his misfortunes, Job wrestled interiorly, seeking initially to understand what God's reasons might be for allowing him to be afflicted with such pain and suffering.

The questions of "why me?" "what have I done to deserve this?" gave way to the deeper questions that were in reality an attempt to grasp and comprehend the inner heart and mind of God.

Where is the justice of God? Why do the innocent suffer while the wicked prosper?

His personal struggle raised Job to a new level of consciousness; the enigma or paradox experienced within himself came to be recognized as a part of the cosmic question.

In the midst of Job's confusion, God spoke. In effect, he said, "Who do you think you are?"

God's response was not one of self-defense nor did it offer a facile solution to the paradox. Through the unanswerable questions that God put to Job, he led him to the self-discovery of his own human limitations.

God's questions pointed to the unfathomable wisdom and greatness revealed in creation.

Overcome with wonder before the greatness of God, Job surrendered.

His former knowledge "by hearsay" had been surpassed in his personal encounter with God. Astounded, Job easily let go of his previous inadequate assumptions about God. No longer reliant on his own strength and integrity, his fears were dissipated. Inspired with a new confidence, Job accepted his human limitations.

Job acknowledged that, before God's wisdom, his own wisdom was ignorance; before God's power, his power was weakness; before the justice of God, the justice of Job was unfairness, and in the light of God's love, his own loving was revealed in all its pettiness.

Job accepted the world as it was in reality, and through that acceptance, he received God as God (46, p. 441).

God is God, and Job is Job.

SUGGESTED APPROACH TO PRAYER:

+ Daily prayer pattern, pages 1 and 2.
    I quiet myself and relax in the presence of God.
    I declare my dependency on God.

+ Grace: I ask for a growing and intense sorrow for sin, even for the gift of tears.

+ Method: Meditation as on page 2.
    I prayerfully reread the passage. I allow the words of Job's surrender to resonate deeply within myself.

    As I meditate on this passage in the light of my own human limitations and sinfulness, I consider the great contrast between God and myself, for example:

God's wisdom — and my need to have all the answers . . . my constant struggle to compensate for my lack of wisdom by impressing others with my knowledge, my degrees, my facts;

God's justice — and my self righteousness and blind oppression of others . . . my hypocritical patterns of over-consumption while criticizing and judging the injustice of others;

God's power — and my misuse and corruption of the authority and influence with which I have been entrusted . . . my grasping to manipulate and control people and situations . . . my hunger for prestige;

God's love — and my envy and suspicious lack of trust . . . my giving with "strings attached" . . . my harsh and petty words and actions;

+ Closing: I go before Jesus crucified, confiding to him the feelings and desires that arise within me and whatever else I am prompted to tell him. I close with an Our Father.

+ Review of Prayer:
    I write in my journal awareness and feelings experienced in the reflection on the contrasts between God and myself.

EZ. 36:25-29

> *I shall pour clean water over you and you will be cleansed.*
> *I shall cleanse you of all your defilement and all your idols.*
> *I shall give you a new heart, and put a new spirit in you; I*
> *shall remove the heart of stone from your bodies and give you*
> *a heart of flesh instead. I shall put my spirit in you, and make*
> *you keep my laws and sincerely respect my observances. You*
> *will live in the land which I gave your ancestors. You shall be*
> *my people and I will be your God. I shall rescue you from all*
> *your defilement. I shall summon the corn and make it plentiful,*
> *and no more bring famines on you.*

COMMENTARY:

The Lord Yahweh speaks:
I will cleanse you;
I shall pour water over you;
I shall give you a new heart;
I shall remove your heart of stone;
I shall put my spirit in you.
It is through and in the holiness of God that Ezekiel shows us God's commitment to restore his people and thereby to reestablish himself among the nations as the compassionate One who cares and has the power to rescue.

God was speaking to the Israelite people who were in exile. They were in a strange land, separated from all they knew and all that gave meaning to their lives. Not only had their land been overtaken by a foreign power, but their homes and businesses, which they had been forced to leave, were taken over by strangers whom the foreign ruler had imported to re-populate the land.

Although they were without their homeland and no longer a political power, the greatest sadness of the exiled people lay in the knowledge that their temple, the center of their religious beliefs, had been burned to the ground.

Previously they had lived their lives out of the limited conception that Yahweh's presence was identified with the land and was focused within the temple.

Living among a pagan people, they were deprived of all the familiar and cultural supports which had nurtured them and from which they had gained their own identity and meaning.

The traumatic experience of exile was viewed by them as the consequence and punishment for their unfaithfulness to God and their unfaithfulness to the covenant promise they had entered into with him.

However, what appeared to be the end of everything became, instead, a new beginning.

Under the leadership of the priest Ezekiel, who had come into exile with them, their experience of displacement became a vehicle for a new vision (Ez 1:4-28).

Ezekiel had carried into exile the sacred scrolls on which were recorded their stories and history. Under his direction they recalled those stories and re-appropriated in faith the dynamic death / life circumstances in which they found themselves.

They looked within their hearts and found there the questions:
 — what are we doing here?
 — where is our God now?
 — to what are we being called?

In the midst of their searching, plunged into the abyss of the pain of their own nothingness, they were wrenched free by a new vision of God.

God spoke, and they heard. They heard **their** God, the God of Abraham, Isaac and Jacob speaking a new promise.

"I will give you a new heart and a new spirit."

The God who spoke to the Israelite people in exile is the same God who speaks to us. And his message remains constant: He is **our** God and we are his people.

God speaks to us in **our** exile. We, as a people, have our own experience of homelessness. It permeates our entire society and is depicted in our contemporary songs and stories.

It was poignantly captured in the tender figure of E.T., in the pathos of his longing to return home. Millions viewed this film and wept, identifying with E.T.'s longing for "home."

Home, in this sense, carries the fuller dimension of being in harmony with our deepest selves, with each other, with our earth, with God.

All of who we are — historically and physically — moves us toward harmony. Where our personal choices and decisions counteract that movement, we experience a radical homelessness/exile of alienation that is the core of sin.

In spite of our human frailty and our personal and communal history of sin, God always stands ready to act in and through the human heart.

The human heart, rather than the head, was for the Hebrews, the center of thought and decision. It is in the knowing, valuing, and choosing of the human heart that God acts, and moves forward the harmony and fruitfulness of our world. In the submission to God's active will, the human heart becomes the new temple of the holiness of God.

For us, as for the exiled people, the "new creation is dependent on our willingness to choose life — to say yes to taking on the task the God of history puts before us" (53, p. 394).

SUGGESTED APPROACH TO PRAYER:

+ Daily prayer pattern, pages 1 and 2.
    I quiet myself and relax in the presence of God.
    I declare my dependency on God.

+ Grace: I ask God for the gift of a growing and intense sorrow for my sins, even of tears.

+ Method: Prayerfully I reread the passage from Ezekiel, allowing God's reassuring words to wash over me.

    I consider how, in spite of my sinfulness, God has supported and given me life to this very moment. I consider how he continues to renew my heart
    — through the beauty and life systems of the earth — air, water, soil;
    — through the enjoyment and service of the great variety of plants and animals;

— through the goodness, love and prayer of people: family, friends, saints. . . .

I consider, finally, with amazement, the paradox of this: that I am a sinner, unfaithful in so many ways, yet, at the same time, I am the recipient of so much goodness and love.

+ Closing: I place myself before Jesus crucified and let my heart speak. I give thanks for his great mercy to me. I close my prayer with an Our Father.

+ Review of Prayer:

I write in my journal any feelings, experiences or insights that have come to my awareness during this prayer period.

PSALM 51

Have mercy on me, O God, in your goodness,
in your great tenderness wipe away my faults;
wash me clean of my guilt,
purify me from my sin.

For I am well aware of my faults,
I have my sin constantly in mind,
having sinned against none other than you,
having done what you regard as wrong.

You are just when you pass sentence on me,
blameless when you give judgment.
You know I was born guilty,
a sinner from the moment of conception.

Yet, since you love sincerity of heart,
teach me the secrets of wisdom.
Purify me with hyssop until I am clean;
wash me until I am whiter than snow.

Instill some joy and gladness into me,
let the bones you have crushed rejoice again.
Hide your face from my sins,
wipe out all my guilt.

God, create a clean heart in me,
put into me a new and constant spirit,
do not banish me from your presence,
do not deprive me of your holy spirit.

Be my savior again, renew my joy,
keep my spirit steady and willing;

and I shall teach transgressors the way to you,
and to you the sinners will return.

Save me from death, God my savior,
and my tongue will acclaim your righteousness;
Lord, open my lips,
and my mouth will speak out your praise.

Sacrifice gives you no pleasure,
were I to offer holocaust, you would not have it.
My sacrifice is this broken spirit,
you will not scorn this crushed and broken heart.

Show your favor graciously to Zion,
rebuild the walls of Jerusalem.
Then there will be proper sacrifice to please you
— holocaust and whole oblation —
and young bulls to be offered on your altar.

COMMENTARY:

This psalm is truly a prayer of the heart, rising from the innermost being of one who has personally experienced the harsh realities of his or her sinfulness.

The psalm expresses a keen awareness of the ramifications that have occurred as a result of personal sin. It reveals a deep need and longing for spiritual cleansing and forgiveness.

Commonly known as the **Miserere**, Psalm 51 is the fourth of the seven penitential psalms. It has been used for centuries in the penitential liturgies of the church.

Traditionally, it has been identified as the prayer / lament of David as he pleaded forgiveness for his sin with Bathsheba. It comes, however, in its present form, from a later time, beautifully rendering the wisdom and hopes of Jeremiah and Ezekiel, prophets of the Exile.

Timeless in its images of yearning, it holds for 20th century men and women, an expression of the contemporary orientation toward the integration of the physical, psychological and spiritual dimensions of self.

It has been a source of consolation and guidance for many in their personal passage from the despair of sin to the joy of forgiveness, from fragmentation to wholeness.

The psalm begins with an image-laden plea for mercy and forgiveness.

In its English translation, the psalm loses some of its impact. The Hebrew text reveals three specific types of sins being confessed: conscious rebellion, translated as "faults," the sin or error, translated as "guilt' and sin as a "going astray," translated simply as "sin."

Paralleling the three areas of sinfulness we hear the psalmist make three pleas for forgiveness in a triple image of cleansing. He prays that his sins of rebellion may be "wiped away," that his sins of error be "washed away" and that his sins of going astray may be "purified."

Once again the imagery is dulled in the English translation. The "wiping away" as well as the "purifying" refer to the temple rituals and ceremonial declarations of forgiveness and/or innocence. The particular Hebraic word used for "washing" has the connotation of vigorous scrubbing such as the Israelite women did when washing their clothes by beating them with stones in cold water (68, p. 258). The psalmist clearly relates a sincere desire for interior cleansing!

Verses three and four echo the beautiful passage of Exodus 34:6-7 where God is described not only as loving but allowing nothing to go unchecked.

God does listen to the plea for mercy. He is faithful; he allows the effects of sin, the alchemy of suffering, to take its transforming course.

Verse five, which states that the sinner was guilty from the moment of conception, is not a commentary on the morality of sexuality, nor does it allude to the doctrine of original sin. Rather, the intended meaning is to convey the tendency all of us as humans have toward rebellion, error and inadequacy.

"Yet since you love sincerity of heart, teach me the secrets of wisdom."

The connection of verse six with verse five is made clear if we hear an alternate translation: "indeed you take pleasure in fidelity amid [conjugal] intimacy; in such secret acts you import the experience of [wondrous] wisdom" (Ibid, p. 259).

Just as new life is conceived in the intimacy of conjugal union, so too, new birth, spiritual renewal is conceived when the heart of the sinner becomes receptive to God's life-giving power.

The remainder of the psalm continues in its plea for forgiveness and renewal. It is permeated with trust and the anticipation of joy.

The psalmist desires to be so appalled at this sinfulness that he will forever be purged of entertaining even the mere idea of sinning again!

He turns to the Lord, asking that he be given the grace of healing that was symbolized in the sprinkling with hyssop. Hyssop is a fragrant, medicinal herb that was commonly used in ritual cleansing. With that healing the psalmist is hopeful that his interior anguish, which he undoubtedly is experiencing even in his body as a crushing weight, will be lifted.

". . . my sacrifice is this broken spirit. . . ."

Only in the recesses of a heart broken open with sorrow and filled with determination can authentic healing and joy be given birth. Without this interior ripening and mature commitment, all the ritual of organized religion is empty.

"Create a clean heart in me, O God."

Psalm 51, in its totality, is a cry for wholeness and it announces a new beginning. The word "create", bará, is the same word used in the first creation account found in Genesis. The energy that was the pulsating force of cosmic creation is the same regenerative force present in the repentant and healed heart.

In this "rebirthing" the integration of self is realized and rooted in the God of compassion. It finds its expression of praise in word and service.

SUGGESTED APPROACH TO PRAYER:

+ Daily prayer pattern, pages 1 and 2.
> I quiet myself and relax in the presence of God.
> I declare my dependency on God.
+ Grace: I ask for the grace of intense sorrow for all my sins.
+ Method: Meditation as on page 2.

I prayerfully read the psalms, aloud if possible, as if the words were my own. I allow the yearning within my heart to find expression through the words of the psalmist. I linger with the verses which speak most profoundly.

+ Closing: I go before Christ crucified and tell him of my yearnings for healing and peace. I close my prayer with an Our Father.

+ Review of Prayer:

I write in my journal the words of the Psalm that have most deeply expressed my own longings.

SUGGESTED APPROACH TO PRAYER:

+ Daily prayer pattern, pages 1 and 2.

    I quiet myself and relax in the presence of God.

    I declare my dependency on God.

+ Grace: I ask for a growing and intense sorrow for my sins, even for the gift of tears.

+ Method: Repetition, as on page 6.

    In preparation, I review my previous prayer periods by reading my journal since the last repetition day. I select for my repetition the period of prayer in which I was most deeply moved, or the one in which I experienced dryness, that is, a lack of emotional response. I use the method with which I approached the passage initially. I open myself to hear again God's word to me in that particular passage.

+ Review of Prayer:

    I write in my journal any feelings, experiences, or insights that have surfaced in this "second listening."

the roots
of
personal
sinfulness

MATTHEW 25:31-46

'When the Son of Man comes in his glory, escorted by all the
angels, then he will take his seat on his throne of glory. All
the nations will be assembled before him and he will separate
[people] one from another as the shepherd separates sheep from
goats. He will place the sheep on his right hand and the goats
on his left. Then the King will say to those on his right hand,
"Come, you whom my Father has blessed, take for your heritage
the kingdom prepared for you since the foundation of the world.
For I was hungry and you gave me food; I was thirsty and you
gave me drink; I was a stranger and you made me welcome;
naked and you clothed me, sick and you visited me, in prison
and you came to see me." Then the virtuous will say to him
in reply, "Lord, when did we see you hungry and feed you;
or thirsty and give you drink? When did we see you a stranger
and make you welcome; naked and clothe you; sick or in prison
and go to see you?" And the King will answer, "I tell you
solemnly, in so far as you did this to one of the least of these
brothers of mine, you did it to me." Next he will say to those
on his left hand, "Go away from me, with your curse upon
you, to the eternal fire prepared for the devil and his angels.
For I was hungry and you never gave me food; I was thirsty
and you never gave me anything to drink; I was a stranger and
you never made me welcome, naked and you never clothed me,
sick and in prison and you never visited me." Then it will be
their turn to ask, "Lord, when did we see you hungry or thirsty,
a stranger or naked, sick or in prison, and did not come to
your help?" Then he will answer, "I tell you solemnly, in so
far as you neglected to do this to one of the least of these, you
neglected to do it for me." And they will go away to eternal
punishment, and the virtuous to eternal life.

COMMENTARY:

This passage brings to mind a woman in northwestern Minnesota who is known and loved by many.

As a child she knew poverty. Housing was inadequate and food was sometimes scarce. Even as a child, she decided that when she grew up, she would find a way to care for the poor.

That decision has influenced and given direction to her entire adult life and commitment. Daily she is involved with serving the needs of the poor. She, and others who have joined her, provide food, clothing, shelter, as well as hope, to the many who come to her in their need.

The decision to actively love those in need is at the heart of this passage. On that decision rests our ultimate judgment. Our saying "yes" to love is saying "yes" to our own fullness in Christ.

This passage is one of the final instructions of Jesus to his disciples, shortly before entering into his passion. He told them that in order to enter into union with Him, they must be engaged in actively meeting the needs of others, particularly the poor and oppressed. This is the theme also found in St. John's presentation of Jesus' farewell message to his disciples (Jn. 13ff).

Although given to the inner circle of disciples, the directive is of universal import; it is meant for "all nations," all people. It is timeless in its scope and relevance.

Each of us is faced daily with the needs of those around us.

The woman mentioned earlier might appear to have an extraordinary commitment to loving the poor. She does. However, if we were to view life from the perspective of this passage, we would begin to see that our lives, too, are extraordinary.

The commitment of marriage, parenthood, profession, etc., is **extra**-ordinary! Within each life commitment we are faced with the daily needs of the people to whom we are committed. Their "poverty," i.e., their brokenness and limitations, are a call to love.

The poverty of those around us in ordinary circumstances may be less dramatic, but, by that fact, more demanding.

Jesus calls us to love in the simple things; it is an uncalculating love, free of self interest, the spontaneous response of a loving heart.

In the passage, Jesus relates to us that when we respond in love, we are responding to Him. We are not responding **as though** He were present, but to his **actual** presence. Jesus has so identified Himself with the poor and suffering that, in the deepest sense, He is present within their suffering, and is the recipient of the love that is extended.

This revelation is as astonishing to us as it was to his first disciples. It is a mysterious, wondrous occurrence that in people loving each other, Christ is recognized and served.

Although the Christ in this passage is exalted and glorified — "the Son of Man" — the paradox is that His is the exaltation of one who identifies with the poor.

If we could hear the message, if it were truly accepted and assimilated, it would turn the world upside down! It challenges our contemporary value system which has as its major collective thrust ego achievement and success.

We have been preoccupied with perfection — "our exultation." This preoccupation has deprived us of wholeness and plummeted us into the self-made hell that is separation from ourselves, from each other, and from God.

If the presence of Christ in each other is astonishing, no less so is the fact that each of us has been given the freedom to make the choices which lead to the discovery of completeness and His presence within.

Too often, however, we have used as an excuse our "fate," i.e., the circumstances of our life. We have allowed ourselves to be programmed and fixated into inflexible patterns. The excuse is a denial of courage.

Jesus did not accept the excuses of those who were separated and on his left, and he will not accept our excuses.

He will, however, accept us with our brokenness and limitations. We need to claim the courage present within us to abandon ourselves with trust to his love and creative grace.

As followers of Jesus and believers in his resurrection, we dare not allow our freedom to be restricted or predetermined by whatever suffering and limitation we encounter. Past inadequate decisions and sinful responses, our own and those of others, cannot be an excuse and need not be an obstacle to fullness of life.

It is a false assumption that the past predetermines us. To live out of that belief is to choose debilitation, destruction and death.

Within our poverty, we stand in a free structure. To reject that freedom is to reject Christ and that is sin!

This passage places upon each Christian the personal responsibility to choose to follow the directives of the Christ of the poor, i.e., to love. Only in choosing to love do we recognize Jesus and realize life.

SUGGESTED APPROACH TO PRAYER:

+ Daily prayer pattern, pages 1 and 2.
    I quiet myself and relax in the presence of God.
    I declare my dependency on God.
+ Grace: I ask for a deepening awareness of the roots of my sinfulness, and for a growing sorrow.
+ Method:
    I take my place among the followers of Jesus. I listen intently to his words. I observe his facial expressions as he speaks to us. As I listen I become aware of a day in my life . . . the people I meet — spouse, family, friends, co-workers . . . I am aware of my patterns of interacting with each one. Then I hear Jesus describe the consequences of not loving. And I ask myself, how have I responded? Am I sent to his right hand as one who is deeply aware of and responsive to the real needs of others? Or am I with those dismissed to his left hand? In what ways have I been unaware, and therefore lacking in true love and responsiveness to others?
    How am I being called to love?
    What are the distractions that have preoccupied my attention and served as obstacles to my loving others?
+ Closing: I close my prayer with a threefold conversation:
    I turn to Mary who, with us, forms part of the community of all who have, or do, follow Christ. As mother of Jesus, she holds a special place in the

communion of saints. In my own words, I ask her to obtain for me the gifts of:

— a deep knowledge of my sinfulness and a hatred for sin;
— an insight into the disorder in my life so that I may know how to refashion my life in the spirit of Jesus;
— an awareness of whatever may distract and separate me from Christ, so that I may let go of all that deflects me from him.

I turn to Jesus, begging him to ask the Father in his name for these same gifts for me.

I turn to God the Father, that he who loved us so much that he sent his only Son will gift me with these same graces.

I pray the Our Father.

+ Review of Prayer:

I write in my journal the feelings, experiences and insights that surfaced within me during this period of prayer.

ROMANS 7:14-25

The Law, of course, as we all know, is spiritual; but I am unspiritual; I have been sold as a slave to sin. I cannot understand my own behavior. I fail to carry out the things I want to do, and I find myself doing the very things I hate. When I act against my own will, that means I have a self that acknowledges that the Law is good, and so the thing behaving in that way is not my self but sin living in me. The fact is, I know of nothing good living in me — living, that is, in my unspiritual self — for though the will to do what is good is in me, the performance is not, with the result that instead of doing the good things I want to do, I carry out the sinful things I do not want. When I act against my will, then, it is not my true self doing it, but sin which lives in me.

In fact, this seems to be the rule, that every single time I want to do good, it is something evil that comes to hand. In my inmost self I dearly love God's Law, but I can see that my body follows a different law that battles against the law which my reason dictates. This is what makes me a prisoner of that law of sin which lives inside my body.

What a wretched person I am! Who will rescue me from this body doomed to death? Thanks be to God through Jesus Christ our Lord!

In short, it is I who with my reason serve the law of God, and no less I who serve in my unspiritual self the law of sin.

COMMENTARY:

"Now why did I do that?"
"It just slipped out!"

"I didn't mean to do that!"

Each of us can identify with the Jekyl and Hyde frustration of St. Paul, not doing what he intended and not intending what he did. For us, as for Paul, the predicament is not amusing.

Like Paul, we, too, feel a "restless" spirit within us that acts, at times, contrary to our truer self. It is our shadow self.

Since earliest times, men and women have wrestled with the conflict between good and evil. It is the mystery which religion has sought to unravel, the question philosophers have pondered, the theme of the world's greatest works of art.

In the myths, the dramas, the epics and the novels of every era, we vicariously identify with those ensnared in this web. As in a mirror, we see ourselves reflected.

Perhaps no other poet has so masterfully depicted the psychological subtleties and potential tragedies of this conflict as has Shakespeare.

In OTHELLO, Shakespeare shows us a man caught between the innocent trust of the beautiful Desdemona and the cunning evil of Iago, his plotting subordinate.

Othello allows himself to be tempted by the manipulative innuendos of Iago, who casts seeds of doubt concerning Desdemona's faithfulness.

Othello succumbs. In the belief that her death will rid the earth of an evil influence, Othello strangles Desdemona. Only when it is too late does he realize that he has killed the one person who has loved him without reservation. He recognizes and claims the evil within himself. In anguish he cries out,

> . . . roast me in sulfur!
> Wash me in steep-down gulfs of liquid fire!
>
> O Desdemona! O Desdemona! dead!
> Oh! Oh! Oh!   (Act V sc ii. OTHELLO)

Recently, in the film **Star Wars**, we have seen the forces for good and evil battle for control. Developing technology of special effects, Spielberg has visually demonstrated the stark contrasting realities between good and evil. Good is depicted as translucent light and empowering strength; evil is shown as forboding darkness and satanic control.

This drama is played out in each of our lives. We do have, within us, a shadow self. Contemporary psychology has emphatically recognized and encouraged us to encounter it. If we repress or deny this negative side of ourselves, we become increasingly vulnerable to its influence, as was Othello.

With Paul, we ask, "who will rescue me?"

It is always a temptation to look to the law as a fundamentalist assurance of safety, righteousness and security. Law, which in theory is meant only to support what reason and wisdom show us to be right, does in fact, when viewed as an entity unto itself, cripple and fixate us.

The law cannot save us!

What is saving is not some**thing**, but some **one**.

The consoling and extraordinary reality is that the someone is Jesus, crucified and risen. The mystery is that his Risen Spirit lives in us as the source of our freedom and hope. ". . . it is in him that we live, and move and exist . . ." (Acts 17:28).

SUGGESTED APPROACH TO PRAYER:

+ Daily prayer pattern, pages 1 and 2.

   I quiet myself and relax in the presence of God.

   I declare my dependency on god.

+ Grace: I ask for a deepening awareness of the roots of my sinfulness, and for a growing sorrow.

+ Method:

   I enter into the confession of St. Paul, as I slowly, prayerfully read Romans 7:14-25, allowing the words to penetrate deeply into my awareness, opening my heart to the feelings and images his words give rise to as I make them my own.

+ Closing: I close my prayer with a threefold conversation:

   I turn to Mary who, with us, forms part of the community of all who have followed or do follow Christ. As mother of Jesus, she holds a special place in the communion of saints. In my own words, I ask her to obtain for me the gifts of:

   — a deep knowledge of my sinfulness and a hatred for sin;

77

— an insight into the disorder in my life so that I may know how to refashion my life in the spirit of Jesus;

— an awareness of whatever may distract and separate me from Christ, so that I may let go of all that deflects me from him.

I turn to Jesus, begging him to ask the Father in his name for these same gifts for me.

I turn to God the Father, that he who loved us so much that he sent his only Son will gift me with these same graces.

I pray the Our Father.

+ Review of Prayer:

I record in my journal the feelings, experiences and insights that surfaced during this period of prayer.

I JOHN 2:12-17

I am writing to you, my own children,
whose sins have already been forgiven through his name;
I am writing to you, fathers,
who have come to know the one
who has existed since the beginning;

I am writing to you, young men,
who have already overcome the Evil One;
I have written to you, children,
because you already know the Father;
I have written to you, fathers,
because you have come to know the one
who has existed since the beginning;
I have written to you, young men,
because you are strong and God's word has made its home in you,
and you have overcome the Evil One.
You must not love this passing world
or anything that is in the world.
The love of the Father cannot be
in any [one] who loves the world,
because nothing the world has to offer
— the sensual body,
the lustful eye,
pride in possessions —
could ever come from the Father
but only from the world;
and the world, with all it craves for,
is coming to an end;
but anyone who does the will of God
remains for ever.

COMMENTARY:

"Congratulations, son, I am proud of you. You have made the right choice. It's worth everything you've had to do without; every effort you have made will be rewarded."

If you were at a reception following commencement exercises and mingled among the parents and graduates, you would repeatedly overhear these words of praise. You would be touched with the preciousness of the moment. It is as if all the love and hope the father had held, dreamed of, worked and sacrificed for, had been realized. In his affectionate words of congratulations, we sense the transparent bond between father and son. Our casual eavesdropping has made us privy to a father's unique moment of joy.

The warmth of the father's affirming words to his son is not unlike the spirit and message we hear addressed to an early Christian community by St. John.

As John speaks to all those he has nurtured in the faith, he calls them his own dear children.

Within the assembly, he then focuses on two specific groups who comprise the community. One group is the elders who, not because of their age, but on account of the longer duration of their membership are called "fathers." The newly baptized make up the second group and are called "young men."

Like the father of the graduate, John affirms those he loves. He rejoices in the good work that has been begun in them. He recalls firmly that by placing their trust in Jesus, they have made the best possible choice.

Now he holds before them all the blessings they and the community have received as a consequence of their faith in the name, that is, in the power of Jesus Christ.

In the presence of Jesus, in an intimate relationship with Him, they experience the peace that flows from knowing themselves as forgiven.

In declaring their dependency on God, they are empowered with the strength and ability not only to overcome evil in themselves but to effect goodness in others. Through this union with Christ they grow in an interior knowledge of God whose "word has made its home" in them.

If we were to continue to listen to the father as he spoke to his son at the reception, the words of praise would probably be followed by words of warning.

"Be careful, remember all you've learned. It is not going to be easy out there in the real world."

This is precisely what John is saying to the community. He is warning them about the "world." "You must not love this passing world."

John's use of the word "world" needs to be explored.

John is **not** implying that Christians do not and should not love the world in which they live. God created the entire universe, the earth and all it contains out of his immense love. The world is good. Jesus himself cherished a loving regard for nature, often drawing on the images of the world for his parables and teachings.

We need to keep in mind while reading John that his use of the word "world" carried a negative connotation. The Greek word was "kosmos" and the word had gradually taken on the burden of a negative moral value. It implied the world as alienated and separated from God.

"By the world is . . . meant that spirit of vanity and malice which transforms into an instrument of sin those human energies intended for the service of God . . ." and humankind (1, para. 37, p. 235).

For John, the choice is very clear. It is as if he is saying, "You can't have it both ways. It is either God or the 'world.' You must choose!"

Apart from God, the world is contaminated. As a part of the world, we, too, have been exposed to and share in that process of degeneracy. While our basic instincts are good and essential to our well being, they are, at the same time, specific areas of vulnerability.

There is within each of us a tendency to excess and exaggeration, particularly in regard to our pursuit of pleasure, our grasping for power and in our accumulation of possessions.

John speaks of these three areas of vulnerability as "sensual body, lustful eye, pride in possession." This is John's understanding of the "world" against which he warns his community.

It is impossible for us to quarantine and isolate ourselves from our own humanness and from the world in which we live.

Our only shield of protection can come from the surrendering to and total acceptance of God's love and grace as it comes to us through Christ.

SUGGESTED APPROACH TO PRAYER:

+ Daily prayer pattern, pages 1 and 2.
   I quiet myself and relax in the presence of God.
   I declare my dependency on God.
+ Grace: I ask God for a deepening awareness of the roots of my sinfulness and for a growing sorrow.
+ Method: As I reread slowly the letter of John, I experience him addressing his words to me, inviting me to reflect on the ways in which I have been affected by the "world" in which I live.

I consider how I have participated and contributed to the disorder and corruption that characterize a world separated from God.

Keeping in mind the three areas of vulnerability that John refers to — pursuit of pleasure, the grasp for power and the accumulation of possessions — I reflect on the following list to be able to identify in myself the behavioral patterns that reveal to me any underlying dispositions or even predispositions that I may have toward more serious sins.

I keep in perspective that it is in the small things of daily life that the erosion of character and attitudes begins. "Some of the things we would do well to meditate on are: impatience, coarseness, uncleanliness, cheap literature, talkativeness, laughing at the faults of others, petty egotism in everyday life, petty enmities, over-sensitiveness, wasting time, cowardice; lack of respect for holy things, harmful spite portraying itself as a clever joke, stubbornness and obstinacy, moodiness that others must put up with, disorder in work, postponement of the unpleasant, gossip, conceit and self-praise, unjust preference for certain people that we find quite pleasant, hastiness in judging, false self-satisfaction, laziness, the tendency to give up learning any more, the tendency to refuse to listen to others . . ." (59, p. 61).

. . . compulsive, excess buying, over-eating / over-drinking, always needing to be best / first / right, preoccupation with appearance, bad manners, sleezy magazines and trashy television, negative / excessive / petty criticism, uncontrollable and / or manipulative anger, masked hostilities, sexist language and / or attitudes. . . .

+ Closing: I close my prayer with a threefold conversation:

I turn to Mary who, with us, forms part of the community of all who have followed or do follow Christ. As mother of Jesus, she holds a special place in the communion of saints. In my own words, I ask her to obtain for me the gifts of:

— a deep knowledge of my sinfulness and a hatred for sin;
— an insight into the disorder in my life so that I may know how to refashion my life in the spirit of Jesus;
— an awareness of whatever may distract and separate me from Christ, so that I may let go of all that deflects me from him.

I turn to Jesus, begging him to ask the Father in his name for these same gifts for me.

I turn to God the Father, that he who loved us so much that he sent his only Son will gift me with these same graces.

I pray the Our Father.

+ Review of Prayer:

After reflecting prayerfully on John's words and the list of sinful behavior patterns, I record in my journal the tendencies I have toward certain areas of sinfulness. I take particular note of those that had not occurred to me previously.

JAMES 1:13-18

Never, when you have been tempted, say, "God sent the temptation"; God cannot be tempted to do anything wrong, and he does not tempt anybody. Everyone who is tempted is attracted and seduced by his own wrong desire. Then the desire conceives and gives birth to sin, and when sin is fully grown, it too has a child, and the child is death.

Make no mistake about this, my dear [people]; it is all that is good, everything that is perfect, which is given to us from above; it comes down from the Father of all light; with him there is no such thing as alteration, no shadow of a change. By his own choice he made us his children by the message of the truth so that we should be a sort of first fruits of all that he had created.

COMMENTARY:

James speaks to us of how sin makes its insidious entry into our lives and can ultimately destroy us.

A poignant commentary on this passage has been offered to us by a woman who recalls her painful journey through addiction and into new life.

"To take the very first sip of wine? There was excitement, desire and curiosity. The wine sparkled in the crystal goblet and those around were drinking comfortably.

"I, too, sipped the wine. It was warm. I drained the glass. What comfort. It was wonderful; I no longer felt depressed! I was giddy with happiness.

"After dinner, I drank more wine and found myself "high" and funny! What power I had to make the others laugh with my funny words — I, who as my usual depressed self, was never funny.

"I learned a twofold lesson that night: wine relieves depression and gives one power.

"That first drink of wine was pure innocence; what would come of it, no one would have guessed.

"So powerful was the lesson, that I wanted to repeat it. I did not want to deal with the depression or its cause. I was evading the roots of the problem that had begun as someone else's mistake, a sin foisted on a young child.

"Yet that mistake and that sin had continued to haunt me in my young adulthood. It came as denial, depression and unhappiness. How would I escape? Relief seemed to lie in the direction of suicide, or the wine gulped to achieve a "high."

"The seduction of the wine was the need for an instant and easy relief from the pain of living with unresolved hate, hurt and guilt. Nothing better came along.

"Soon, very soon, the ravages of alcoholism caught me in a tidal wave of destruction. God would not help me, I said, since **He** didn't care. God was a "He" and I had been crushed by a "he."

"It was not wrong for me to desire peace within my heart instead of the civil wars that raged there. My methods to attain serenity were wrong — I turned from alcohol to tranquilizers, to pain pills. Addicted to these outside forces and under their control, I was being propelled toward a premature death.

"Gradually the drugs quit working for me. They turned on me. I got more and more depressed. Not only could one not trust God, parents or friends . . . even drugs betrayed me.

"I came as close to death at my own hands as I ever care to. The child of alcoholism is death: spiritual, emotional and physical death. I almost completed the latter and had already experienced the first two.

"When I awoke in an ICU bed and was told I was "lucky" to be alive, something took hold inside of me. In the previous night with the waves of pain from the overdose and the thought that I was dying, I had said to myself, "Well, **you** did this — **you** did it — are you ready to die?"

"Finally, I took responsibility for my life and possible death.

"As I recuperated over the next few weeks, I let God into my life. I said, "Who am I to say that God does not care for me? Let him decide."

"From those first faltering steps back to the Light, growth has occurred in direct proportion to my relationship with God. On the road to recovery, I became aware of God's faithfulness. God is always there — ready to help, to heal, always loving us.

"Serenity, peace and calmness are now more the rule and the civil wars are over. I dealt with the source of the depression and the God of healing, who forgives all sin, graced me with forgiveness for those in my life who had injured me.

"I need not be devastated for life because of someone else's mistakes and sins. What freedom!"

SUGGESTED APPROACH TO PRAYER:

+ Daily prayer pattern, pages 1 and 2.
>   I quiet myself and relax in the presence of God.
>   I declare my dependency on God.

+ Grace: I ask for a keen awareness of the roots of my sinfulness, and for a growing sorrow.

+ Method: I prayerfully reread the words of James.
>   I become aware of an area of sinfulness in my life, recalling from the past the first instances of seduction and how it has grown like a virus and infected so many aspects of my life . . . ministry, self esteem, prayer, relationships, etc.

+ Closing: I close my prayer with a threefold conversation:
>   I turn to Mary who, with us, forms part of the community of all who have followed or do follow Christ. As mother of Jesus, she holds a special place in the communion of saints. In my own words, I ask her to obtain for me the gifts of:
>   — a deep knowledge of my sinfulness and a hatred of sin;
>   — an insight into the disorder in my life so that I may know how to refashion my life in the spirit of Jesus;
>   — an awareness of whatever may distract and separate me from Christ, so that I may let go of all that deflects me from him.

>   I turn to Jesus, begging him to ask the Father in His Name for these same gifts for me.

>   I turn to God the Father, that he who loved us so much that he sent his only Son will gift me with these same graces.

I pray the Our Father.

+ Review of Prayer:

I record in my journal any new awareness of how seduction to sin has influenced me and how God is drawing me to himself.

JAMES 3:2-12

> *After all, every one of us does something wrong, over and over again; the only [one] who could reach perfection would be someone who never said anything wrong — he would be able to control every part of himself. Once we put a bit into the horse's mouth, to make it do what we want, we have the whole animal under our control. Or think of ships: no matter how big they are, even if a gale is driving them, the man at the helm can steer them anywhere he likes by controlling a tiny rudder. So is the tongue only a tiny part of the body, but it can proudly claim that it does great things. Think how small a flame can set fire to a huge forest; the tongue is a flame like that. Among all the parts of the body, the tongue is a whole wicked world in itself: it infects the whole body; catching fire itself from hell, it sets fire to the whole wheel of creation. Wild animals and birds, reptiles and fish can all be tamed by man, and often are; but nobody can tame the tongue — it is a pest that will not keep still, full of deadly poison. We use it to bless the Lord and Father, but we also use it to curse [others] who are made in God's image: the blessing and the curse come out of the same mouth. My [people], this must be wrong — does any water supply give a flow of fresh water and salt water out of the same pipe? Can a fig tree give you olives, . . . or a vine give figs? No more can sea water give you fresh water.*

COMMENTARY:

Panic ensues throughout the nation when a sniper "cuts loose," killing at random anyone within range. Our country, as well as every other nation, has experienced and become increasingly aware of recurrent waves of terrorism, as violence precipitates violence.

We are, in a sense, being held psychologically at bay, fearing that in an unsuspected moment, a senseless spray of death will be discharged by the deranged will of an insane or fanatic person.

This passage in the letter of James calls our attention to the faculty of speech and how in **its** abuse the tongue becomes a devastating weapon which issues forth its own particular "spray of death" and which incites within us an undeniable fear and alarm.

The tongue can kill.

The tongue has the capacity to cut down or to totally deface a person. With a caustic harshness or sometimes more subtly like a suave smooth knife, it can destroy people's lives, sever relationships, and even split apart entire communities.

The potential death-dealing power of the tongue must not be underestimated.

"Many have fallen by the edge of the sword, but many more have fallen by the tongue . . . the death it inflicts is a miserable death" (Si. 28:18, 21a).

This quotation from Sirach (Ecclesiasticus) strengthens James' denunciation of the misuse of speech.

James makes it clear that we all fall into undisciplined, loose habits of speaking. It happens "over and over."

In using the images of bit and rudder, he illustrates for us the necessity for decisive control. Repeatedly we must elevate to the level of awareness the power of the human tongue and the potential there is for good or evil in the gift of speech.

Just as the rider controls the horse by the bit in the horse's mouth, and just as the pilot guides the course of the ship by the use of the rudder, the will is the self-determining force which gives direction to the tongue.

The will is the means by which we exercise our responsibility in speaking. In assuming that responsibility, in bringing our speech under the direction of our free and conscious choice, every aspect of our lives benefits and results in an increased coordination and focus. As James says, "once we put a bit into the horse's mouth . . . we have the whole animal under control"!

The exercise of the will is key in the integrative, evolutionary process of becoming fully human. To attend to that conscious willing is to offset the pernicious tendencies and randomness that characterizes the innate lack of discipline which haunts us from birth to death.

From the one source comes the potential for good or evil. The speaking of a word immediately releases energy which sets into motion the intended effect, whether good or evil, that is, blessing or curse. James urges us to choose wisely.

To deliberately choose to bless is to save ourselves from the destructive fire which evil ignites and which spreads throughout all of creation.

> *"You have in you a spiritual gift . . . do not let it lie unused. Think hard about all this and put it into practice and everyone will be able to see how you are advancing. Take great care about what you do and what you teach [say]; always do this, and in this way you will save both yourself and those who listen to you."*
>
> (I Tim 4:14 ff.)

In faith, the individual act of will frees the gift of speech for the purpose it was intended — for praise and for blessing.

SUGGESTED APPROACH TO PRAYER:

+ Daily prayer pattern, pages 1 and 2.
> I quiet myself and relax in the presence of God.
> I declare my dependency on God.

+ Grace: I ask God for a deepening awareness of the roots of my sinfulness, and for growing sorrow.

+ Method: In light of the passage in James on the use / abuse of the tongue, and in light of the significance of the will, I prayerfully consider the role and exercise of will in my life, particularly as it relates to speech. I ask God to make me aware of the areas in which I need to be strengthened.

> I begin by taking a look at my will.
> "Is it frequently
>> pushed around by the will of other people?
>> subjugated by my feelings, such as depression, anger or fear?
>> paralyzed by inertia?
>> lulled to sleep by habit?
>> disintegrated by distractions?
>> corroded by doubts?

"Do [I] generally do what [I] wish, from the depths of [my] being, because [I] have willed it, or does some other factor prevail?

"[I will] take some time to consider the major aspects of [my] life and [my] most important relationships. [I will] write down [my] answers in detail."

(from WHAT WE MAY BE by Piero Ferrucci. Copyright ©1983 by Piero Ferrucci. Adapted by permission of J.P. Tarcher, Inc., and Houghton Mifflin Company, p. 74).

I reflect on the patterns of speech on any particular day. Have my words been a blessing or curse?

As I become aware of the disorder of speech in my life and my need to strengthen my will in that regard, I consider, from among the following, an action or actions which would be most appropriate for me.

I will adopt and practice the action(s) on a daily basis until new — and blessed — habits of speech become more natural and spontaneous.

I will say something I have never said before, e.g., a compliment, a thank you, a declaration of love.

I will listen when I am prompted to speak.

I will slow my pattern of speech in order to assure that I am saying what I most want to convey in the manner in which it will be most effectively received.

I will totally abstain from using God's name irreverently and from vulgar language.

I will counteract negative remarks with positive comments or with silence.

I will refrain my overtalkativeness or moody silence.

I will extend a verbal greeting to someone who doesn't appeal to me.

I will say "no" when it is right to say "no" but easier to say "yes."

I will say "yes" when it is right to say "yes" but easier to say "no."

I will gently image beforehand my response to people I will be with.

I will read / recite aloud beautiful scripture passages / prayers / poetry.

I will speak tactfully from my own convictions, independently of what others think, say or expect.

I will communicate to others what is deepest within me, e.g., feelings of anger, love, sadness.

This exercise can be adapted to any disordered area of behavior, by creating for oneself a list of actions that would positively strengthen one's will and facilitate change.

+ Closing: Colloquy

I close my prayer with a threefold conversation:

I turn to Mary who, with us, forms part of the community of all who have followed or do follow Christ. As mother of Jesus, she holds a special place in the communion of saints. In my own words, I ask her to obtain for me the gifts of:

— a deep knowledge of my sinfulness and a hatred for sin;
— an insight into the disorder in my life so that I may know how to refashion my life in the spirit of Jesus;
— an awareness of whatever may distract and separate me from Christ, so that I may let go of all that deflects me from him.

I turn to Jesus, begging him to ask the Father in His Name for these same gifts for me.

I turn to God the Father, that he who loved us so much that he sent his only Son will gift me with these same graces.

I pray the Our Father.

+ Review of Prayer:

I write in my journal the actions that I have chosen to strengthen my will. I write any feelings or insights which are motivating these choices.

JAMES 4:1-10

> *Where do these wars and battles between yourselves first start?
> Isn't it precisely in the desires fighting inside your own selves?
> You want something and you haven't got it; so you are prepared
> to kill. You have an ambition that you cannot satisfy, so you
> fight to get your way by force. Why you don't have what you
> want is because you don't pray for it; when you do pray and
> don't get it, it is because you have not prayed properly; you
> have prayed for something to indulge your own desires.*

> *You are as unfaithful as adulterous wives; don't you realize
> that making the world your friend is making God your enemy?
> Anyone who chooses the world for his friend turns himself into
> God's enemy. Surely you don't think scripture is wrong when it
> says: the spirit which he sent to live in us wants us for himself
> alone? But he has been even more generous to us, as scripture
> says: God opposes the proud but he gives generously to the
> humble. Give in to God, then; resist the devil, and he will
> run away from you. The nearer you go to God, the nearer
> he will come to you. Clean your hands, you sinners, and clear
> your minds, you waverers. Look at your wretched condition,
> and weep for it in misery; be miserable instead of laughing,
> gloomy instead of happy. Humble yourselves before the Lord
> and he will lift you up.*

COMMENTARY:

We do want what others have.
We do envy the success of others.
We are greedy, always wanting more and more.
We do crave recognition and praise, wanting to be first and to be best.

Our passions gone awry fight within us and wield heavy blows. Without God, there is no way that we are able to withstand their onslaught.

Only by giving in to God, surrendering to the power of goodness can we find peace.

Peace is not detente. To live in detente would be to live in a state of unawareness and of false harmony, in a passivity of mere existence, toleration and denial. We would be subject to and live in fear of inexplicable and unpredictable eruptions from within.

The challenge is to face and to confront our inner selves. Unless we are willing to put forth the prayer, reflection and discipline necessary to grow in self awareness, we will never discover the unconscious motivations behind our words and actions. We will not know why some particular things carry such a weight of importance to us.

In her book, **Addiction to Perfection**, Marian Woodman cautions us on the importance of asking ourselves the right question: "Do I see what I am doing?" (74, 163).

The inclination to be superior to and independent of others is a common human denominator. In whatever arena we find ourselves, and however that superiority seeks expression, its name is pride.

Given our propensity toward egotism, we need to be constantly alert, asking ourselves the questions:

What is the need that triggers the underlying drive within?

How does this action feed my desire to be self-sufficient and independent, not only of others but even of God?

How do the negative effects of my words and actions in the lives of others reveal or mirror my own area of sinfulness? What does their response say to me?

The answers to these questions will enable us to recognize our most authentic self, not only our potential for goodness but also our limitations, brokenness, and sinfulness. We will be led through this self-awareness into a deep mourning as we are forced to accept the reality of the pain our actions have inflicted on others. The new level of consciousness will compel us to relinquish the former ideals and behaviors which have drawn on values extrinsic to the inner value of our truest self. Like idols they have deflected us from God. Unmasked they are seen for what they are — false gods.

94

Do I see what I am doing and why I am doing it?

In an ancient manuscript, Jesus is recorded as saying,

Friend, if you know what you are doing, you are blessed, but if you do not know, you are accursed. . . . (Jerusalem Bible, 101, footnote 6a)

Our God is a God of blessing, and he is yearning to be near us. Scripture gives us a precious analogy of God's love, comparing it to the intimate love between husband and wife.

For James, as for the Old Testament prophets, succumbing to the seduction of false gods was not only a matter of breaking the Law, but of the "breaking of God's heart." It was likened to the sin of adultery.

We belong to God. He loves us with a total love. His desire is that we respond with our whole selves, body, mind and heart (Mt. 22:37-38). Like a devoted spouse, God will not share us with other gods.

"They have roused me to jealousy with what is no god, they have angered me with their beings of nothing" (Dt. 32:21a).

"Give in to God." To respond in love is to surrender; to surrender to the God of love is to pray always.

To pray is to breathe deeply of the life-giving breath which God gave us at birth. Like life itself, prayer is an entry into a love rhythm:

the rhythm of God's nurturing love and our childlike dependency;

the rhythm of God's forgiving love and our tears; and

the rhythm of God's intimate love and our transparent receptivity.

"Humble yourselves before the Lord and He will lift you up."

SUGGESTED APPROACH TO PRAYER:

+ Daily prayer pattern, pages 1 and 2.

I quiet myself and relax in the presence of God.

I declare my dependency on God.

+ Grace: I draw near to God, asking for the gift to see clearly my own sinfulness and to be sincerely sorry.

+ Method: Mantra as on page 4.

"The nearer you go to God, the nearer he will come to you."

I center by using these words as a mantra. As I breathe out, I will say softly, "the nearer I go to God," and breathing, I will say, "the nearer he will come to me."

+ Closing: I close my prayer with a threefold conversation:

I turn to Mary who, with us, forms part of the community of all who have followed or do follow Christ. As mother of Jesus, she holds a special place in the communion of saints. In my own words, I ask her to obtain for me the gifts of:

— a deep knowledge of my sinfulness and a hatred for sin;
— an insight into the disorder in my life so that I may know how to refashion my life in the spirit of Jesus;
— an awareness of whatever may distract and separate me from Christ, so that I may let go of all that deflects me from him.

I turn to Jesus, begging him to ask the Father in His Name for these same gifts for me.

I turn to God the Father, that he who loved us so much that he sent his only Son will gift me with these same graces.

I pray the Our Father.

+ Review of Prayer:

I write in my journal any feelings I had while praying the mantra.

LUKE 12:16-21

> *Then he told them a parable. "There was once a rich man who,*
> *having had a good harvest from his hand, thought to himself,*
> *'What am I to do? I have not enough room to store my crops.'*
> *Then he said, 'This is what I will do: I will pull down my barns*
> *and build bigger ones, and store all my grain and my goods in*
> *them, and I will say to my soul: My soul, you have plenty of*
> *good things laid by for many years to come; take things easy,*
> *eat, drink, have a good time.' But God said to him, 'Fool! This*
> *very night the demand will be made for your soul; and this*
> *hoard of yours, whose will it be then?' So it is when [anyone]*
> *stores up treasure for himself in place of making himself rich*
> *in the sight of God."*

COMMENTARY:

Isn't this a boring story? All we hear from the farmer is what he has, how great his crop is, what he has done and the good time he is going to have.

Thank goodness, God speaks!

God's words pierce through the false security of the rich man's plan.

God calls him a fool! Poor man, he had spent his entire life anxiously gathering, building and storing. And now, just at the point when he could indulge himself, God tells him that he is bankrupt. The man is spiritually bankrupt, not rich at all in God's eyes.

The story about the rich man and God's response serves as an example for what our attitude should be toward material possessions. It cautions us not to place our security in them.

The relevance of the passage is strikingly apparent. In contemporary society there is an overwhelming tendency to identify ourselves and each other with what we have. The word "security" is most frequently interpreted as meaning financial security. As a result, most of our energy and time is spent in the frantic pursuit of it.

The high incidence of stress-related illnesses in our culture lays bare the hidden truth of just how totally we have taken on this futile striving, collectively as well as individually. It is an unending, escalating struggle which, for some, literally ends in physical death. Others, while alive, become paralyzed in self-centered fixation.

As strong a case as Luke presents, the intent is not to condemn material possession. Nor can the passage be used to condone a life of laziness or irresponsible dependency.

Neither can the meaning of this passage be limited to its interpretation as a warning in regard to our impending death and final judgment. There is a fuller meaning.

We are being alerted to the reality that our judgment is taking place **now**. Within our own hearts we are being judged by the Spirit.

The judgment is tragic if we are guilty of neglecting and closing ourselves off to the Kingdom which is already present within us and totally accessible at every moment.

The greatest sadness is not death; it is to have missed life.

That is the tragedy of the rich man of this parable.

> *We have been given possession of an unshakable kingdom.*
> *Let us therefore hold on to the grace that we have been given*
> *and use it to worship God in the way that he finds acceptable,*
> *in reverence and fear. (Heb 12:28)*

SUGGESTED APPROACH TO PRAYER:

+ Daily prayer pattern, pages 1 and 2.

    I quiet myself and relax in the presence of God.

    I declare my dependency on God.

+ Grace: I ask for a growing awareness of my sinfulness and for deepening sorrow.

+ Method: After recalling the parable,

I listen carefully to the Spirit within me. I focus on a particular disorder, the one that emerges as the most apparent, basic and insidious. I ask for the grace to recognize how this disorder is expressed by the consideration of the following questions:

What is it that I gather? — riches, degrees, prestige . . . ?

What have I built to house my "treasures"? — roles, positions, buildings . . . ?

What have I stored up as my security for the future? — reputation, wealth, power, relationships . . . ?

+ Closing: I close my prayer with a threefold conversation:

I turn to Mary who, with us, forms part of the community of all who have followed or do follow Christ. As mother of Jesus, she holds a special place in the communion of saints. In my own words, I ask her to obtain for me the gifts of:

— a deep knowledge of my sinfulness and a hatred for sin;
— an insight into the disorder in my life so that I may know how to refashion my life in the spirit of Jesus;
— an awareness of whatever may distract and separate me from Christ, so that I may let go of all that deflects me from him.

I turn to Jesus, begging him to ask the Father in His Name for these same gifts for me.

I turn to God the Father, that he who loved us so much that he sent his only Son will gift me with these same graces.

I pray the Our Father.

+ Review of Prayer:

I write in my journal my responses to the questions posed, as well as any feelings that surfaced during the period of prayer.

MARK 7:1-23

The Pharisees and some of the scribes who had come from Jerusalem gathered around him, and they noticed that some of his disciples were eating with unclean hands, that is, without washing them. For the Pharisees, and the Jews in general, follow the tradition of the elders and never eat without washing their arms as far as the elbow; and on returning from the market place they never eat without first sprinkling themselves. There are also many other observances which have been handed down to them concerning the washing of cups and pots and bronze dishes. So these Pharisees and scribes asked him, "Why do your disciples not respect the tradition of the elders but eat their food with unclean hands?" He answered, "It was of you hypocrites that Isaiah so rightly prophesied in this passage of scripture:

> *This people honors me only with lip-service,*
> *while their hearts are far from me.*
> *The worship they offer me is worthless,*
> *the doctrines they teach are only human regulations.*

You put aside the commandment of God to cling to human traditions." And he said to them, "How ingeniously you get around the commandment of God in order to preserve your own tradition! For Moses said: Do your duty to your father and your mother, and, Anyone who curses father or mother must be put to death. But you say, 'If a man says to his father or mother: Anything I have that I might have used to help you is Corban (that is, dedicated to God), then he is forbidden from that moment to do anything for his father or mother.' In this way you make God's word null and void for the sake of your tradition which you have handed down. And you do many other things like this."

He called the people to him again and said, "Listen to me, all of you, and understand. Nothing that goes into a man from outside can make him unclean; it is the things that come out of a person that make him unclean. If anyone has ears to hear, let him listen to this."

When he had gone back into the house, away from the crowd, his disciples questioned him about the parable. He said to them, "Do you not understand either? Can you not see that whatever goes into a [person] from outside cannot make him unclean, because it does not go into his heart but through his stomach and passes out into the sewer?" (Thus he pronounced all foods clean.) And he went on, "It is what comes out of a [person] that makes him unclean. For it is from within, from [human] hearts, that evil intentions emerge: fornication, theft, murder, adultery, avarice, malice, deceit, indecency, envy, slander, pride, folly. All these evil things come from within and make a [person] unclean."

COMMENTARY:

In Mark 7, we find some of the most revolutionary teachings in the New Testament. With prophetic insight, Jesus spoke out against the external practices that had been adopted and endorsed as the essence of religious worship. By word and example, Jesus nullified the system of cultic purity which was based on an archaic concept of what was "clean and unclean."

Tragically, the people had lost sight of the hope and freedom which the Mosaic convenant offered to them. Subject to the oppressive leadership of the scribes and pharisees, they labored under an intolerable weight of rules and regulations.

The essential difference between the teachings of Jesus and the mentality of the pharisees is laid bare in this passage.

The pharisees were a lay group who, historically, stood in opposition to the Jewish priestly class. The name pharisee means "separate"; by their fanaticism for ritual and law, the pharisees had set themselves apart from the rest of society.

In their isolation, their attitude became one of comparison and inflated superiority.

Adherence to the law and tradition was meticulous. Every letter of the law was compulsively obeyed. The pitfall was that what began historically as a sincere effort to renew Judaic faith resulted in an obsessive exaggeration of law. Ironically, the law itself became an obstacle to inner renewal. So much happened externally that nothing took place interiorly. Gradually external practices of the law began to be used as an escape from the deeper obligation and summons of God's command to love:

> You shall love Yahweh your God with all your heart, with all your soul, with all your strength. Let these words . . . be written on your heart.
>
> (Dt 6:5-6)

Appalled by the irrelevancy and masked evil of these excessive practices, Jesus did not spare the pharisees. His condemnation of the hypocrisy perpetrated by these excesses was severe. Hypocrisy — the wearing of a mask — and role playing were totally unacceptable to Jesus. The pharisees, motivated by self-interest and the desire to make a good impression, abused their religious authority and manipulated the sincerity of the people to serve their own advancement.

In this passage, Jesus harshly criticized and accused the pharisees of hypocrisy on two separate charges: the compulsiveness of ritual cleansing and the clever deception of practices like corban.

The heated exchange began when the pharisees challenged Jesus because his disciples did not observe the tradition of washing their hands before eating.

Jesus and the disciples were confronted with traditions of long standing which had taken on the force of law. Orally handed down from generation to genera-tion, these rigid traditions, known as the **Halakak**, were an elaborate body of rules and regulations intended to govern every conceivable action and circumstance.

The directives regulating the ceremonial cleansing of hands and vessels reached absurd proportions. Hands had to be cleansed in a particular manner, and the specific methods for cleansing vessels were determined by the shape, the material and the function of the container.

Angered by the pharisees' efforts to impose their sterile customs on his disciples,

Jesus lashed out and called them hypocrites. He penetrated the protective shield of their self-righteousness by facing them with the contradictory and contemptible reality of their situation. The accusation that centuries earlier Isaiah had leveled at Israel, Jesus now mercilessly applied to the pharisees,

This people honors me only with lip-service,
while their hearts are far from me.
The worship they offer me is worthless,
the doctrines they teach are only human regulations.

Jesus continued to strip away the layers of their sanctimonious affectation. With unerring accuracy and biting sarcasm he delivered judgment: "How ingeniously you get around the commandment of God in order to preserve your own tradition."

His second charge was against a concrete example of their dubious "ingenuity." It addressed the unjust and popular practice of corban.

Originally, corban was a practice of offering one's gifts to God. The gifts were called "corban." By the time of Jesus, the practice of corban had fallen into abuse. The pharisees used it to serve their own interests, to escape real obligations, even to the point of neglecting the care of their aging parents.

Whatever was proclaimed "corban" could not legally be used for other purposes; it belonged to God. A son might say, "I cannot help you because all my money is promised to God." With this formal assertion, the money was not longer available for the care of his parents, even if later he were to retract his promise.

Once again Jesus called on their deeper tradition to witness in the case against the pharisees. He confronted them with the fundamental teaching of Moses, "Do your duty to your father and your mother . . . Anyone who curses father or mother must be put to death."

But Jesus was not yet finished. He went on to say that this was only one case among many in which they had justified their behavior and indulged their insatiable ego appetites for prestige and control.

The price they had paid for this blatant abuse of God's law was the negation of their own innermost spirit; God's word for them had become "null and void." A phenomenal tragedy — they were spiritually blind leaders!

Jesus, moved with compassion, turned to address all the people, inviting them to listen and to understand. The invitation to "all of you" indicated the universality of Jesus' message, and the death of spiritual elitism. The instruction to "understand" signified the importance of the message that followed: Nothing that goes into a man from outside can make him unclean; it is the things that come out of a man that make him unclean.

The message was not only important; it was surprising and new!

In one radical declaration Jesus effectively shattered the rigid moral/ethical structure which was based on distinction of cleanness and uncleanness. Things in themselves were declared neither clean nor unclean, neither good nor bad.

By this declaration Jesus rejected all **superfluous externals**; the traditions, prescriptions, rules and rituals that had come to dominate religious experience were totally dismissed as irrelevant.

Much to Jesus' chagrin, the disciples did not understand this teaching. He took them aside and privately explained it further. The core of his message was that it is within the innermost truth of each individual that one discovers the ultimate rule of love. In the end it is not the external rules that give shape to interior development and personal individuation. Each person is required by Jesus to enter the depths of his/her own heart/consciousness and to discover there an authentic discernment which goes beyond the morality of law. The spiritual quality, the "cleanness" of any outward expression — word or action — of a person is proportionate to the attentiveness to God's spirit within.

SUGGESTED APPROACH TO PRAYER:

+ Daily prayer pattern, pages 1 and 2.
    I quiet myself and relax in the presence of God.
    I declare my dependency on God.
+ Grace: I ask to deepen the awareness of my sinfulness and for a growing sorrow.
+ Method:
    Jesus had harsh words for "hypocrites," a word whose root meaning referred to those who "wear a mask" as actors did in ancient times, to represent the role they were imitating.

I stand before Jesus. He looks at me. I look into his eyes, and there, what do I see reflected?

What are the roles I play? . . . the one who is always right? . . . the one who is in control?

Do I smile outwardly while carrying a grudge within?

I look into the eyes of Jesus as into a mirror, and let appear the masks I wear.

I listen to the words Jesus addressed to the pharisees, as if he were speaking directly to me. What do I learn about myself from the feelings and images his words arouse in me?

+ Closing: I close my prayer with a threefold conversation:

I turn to Mary who, with us, forms part of the community of all who have followed or do follow Christ. As mother of Jesus, she holds a special place in the communion of Saints. In my own words, I ask her to obtain for me the gifts of:

— a deep knowledge of my sinfulness and a hatred for sin:
— an insight into the disorder in my life so that I may know how to refashion my life in the spirit of Jesus;
— an awareness of whatever may distract and separate me from Christ, so that I may let go of all that deflects me from him.

I turn to Jesus, begging him to ask the Father in His Name for these same gifts for me.

I turn to God the Father, that he who loved us so much that he sent his only Son will gift me with these same graces.

I pray the Our Father.

+ Review of Prayer:

I will write in my journal any feelings which were elicited as I listened to Jesus speak to me.

LUKE 18:9-14

> *He spoke the following parable to some people who prided*
> *themselves on being virtuous and despised everyone else,*
> *"Two men went up to the Temple to pray, one a Pharisee,*
> *the other a tax collector. The Pharisee stood there and said*
> *this prayer to himself, 'I thank you, God, that I am not*
> *grasping, unjust, adulterous like the rest of mankind and*
> *particularly that I am not like this tax collector here.*
> *I fast twice a week. I pay tithes on all I get.' The tax*
> *collector stood some distance away, not daring even to*
> *raise his eyes to heaven, but he beat his breast and said,*
> *'God, be merciful to me, a sinner.' This man, I tell you,*
> *went home again at rights with God; the other did not.*
> *For everyone who exalts himself will be humbled, but the*
> *[one] who humbles himself will be exalted."*

COMMENTARY:

The pharisee or the tax collector — who are you?

Contrary to the tendency to identify with one or the other, the greater truth is that within each of us there are the dispositions and attitudes of both the pharisee and the tax collector.

There is something about the pharisee that makes us cringe! In the parable the pharisee is depicted as having pompous superiority. The pharisees were faithful to the law. They did fast; they did pray; they did pay tithes on all they earned. Externally and publicly they observed all the prescribed religious law.

The pharisee of the parable was no exception.

But how was his prayer?

It is amusing to read in the parable that he prayed "to" himself. A closer look discloses that he literally did pray **to himself**!

What began as thanksgiving to God regressed to a self-congratulatory litany of exaggerated holiness. Standing with arms extended, filled with over-confidence, he used the public forum of prayer to fulfill his own neurotic need for recognition. What externally appeared as prayer was, in fact, no prayer.

The stance and expression of the tax collector was a startling contrast to that of the pharisee.

The tax collector took his place at "a distance," his head bowed, his eyes cast down as he pleaded for mercy. His clenched fist against his heart expressed the intensity of his inner anguish. The original text indicates that the tax collector did not think of himself as simply **a** sinner, but as **the** sinner. He had an acute awareness of the depth and extent of his personal sinfulness, of the fraud, the duplicity, the cheating that had shaped his life as a public servant.

With the psalmist he could pray,

> . . . I am well aware of my faults,
> I have my sins constantly in mind,
> having sinned against none other than you. . . .   (Ps 51:3-4a)

In contrast to the prayer of the pharisee, the prayer of the tax collector was humble. He had searched his heart, and he had discovered his guilt. In helplessness he threw himself on God's compassionate love and mercy. It was at the moment of truth and surrender that the tax collector was lifted up.

The difference between the pharisee and the tax collector was sustained to the end of the story. In his self-exultation, the pharisee went away empty. On the other hand, by submitting himself to God's mercy and forgiveness, the tax collector was freed from the binding effects of his sins. His confession of guilt opened to him the deeper reality of himself; it prepared the way for his mature and moral completeness in Christ. ". . . he went home justified."

Jesus closes his teaching simply and directly: Whoever exalts himself will be humbled and whoever humbles himself will be exalted.

SUGGESTED APPROACH TO PRAYER:

+ Daily prayer pattern, pages 1 and 2.
    I quiet myself and relax in the presence of God.
    I declare my dependency on God.

+ Grace: I ask for the grace to deepen the awareness of my sinfulness and for a growing sorrow.

+ Method: Contemplation as on page 3.

I image myself in the temple. I see the temple in great detail, become aware of the crowd of worshippers.

Recognizing that there is within me both the pharisee and the tax collector, I will first assume the role of the pharisee.

I take the position and interior stance of prayer that was his. I pray a similar prayer of superiority which reflects my own attitudes and tendencies toward comparison.

Next, I assume the role, position and interior stance of the tax collector. I pray as he prayed, expressing sorrow and begging God's mercy for **my** sins.

At the end of my contemplation of the pharisee and the tax collector, I ask myself:

What feeling arose within me? What did I learn about myself . . . about my attitudes, my areas of sinfulness, and the depth of my sorrow? Then I listen and watch Jesus as he prays the Our Father.

+ Closing: I close my prayer with a threefold conversation:

I turn to Mary who, with us, forms part of the community of all who have followed or do follow Christ. As mother of Jesus, she holds a special place in the communion of saints. In my own words, I ask her to obtain for me the gifts of:

— a deep knowledge of my sinfulness and a hatred for sin;

— an insight into the disorder in my life so that I may know how to refashion my life in the spirit of Jesus;

— an awareness of whatever may distract and separate me from Christ, so that I may let go of all that deflects me from him.

I turn to Jesus, begging him to ask the Father in His Name for these same gifts for me.

I turn to God the Father, that he who loved us so much that He sent His only Son will gift me with these same graces.

I pray the Our Father.

+ Review of Prayer:

I write in my journal the feelings, experiences and insights that occurred during this period of prayer.

SUGGESTED APPROACH TO PRAYER:

+ Daily prayer pattern, pages 1 and 2.

I quiet myself and relax in the presence of God.

I declare my dependency on God.

+ Grace: I ask for a growing awareness of the root of my sinful disorders and for a deepening sorrow.

+ Method: Repetition as on page 6.

In preparation, I review my previous prayer periods by reading my journal since the last repetition day. I select for my repetition the period of prayer in which I was most deeply moved, or the one in which I experienced dryness, that is, a lack of emotional response. I use the method with which I approached the passage initially. I open myself to hear again God's word to me in that particular passage.

+ Review of Prayer:

I write in my journal any feelings, experiences, or insights that have surfaced in this "second listening."

God's
merciful
forgiveness

LUKE 15:11-32

He also said, "A man had two sons. The younger said to his
father, 'Father, let me have the share of the estate that would
come to me.' So the father divided the property between them.
A few days later, the younger son got together everything
he had and left for a distant country where he squandered
his money on a life of debauchery.

"When he had spent it all, that country experienced a severe
famine, and now he began to feel the pinch, so he hired himself
out to one of the local inhabitants who put him on his farm to
feed the pigs. And he would willingly have filled his belly with
the husks the pigs were eating but no one offered him anything.
Then he came to his senses and said, 'How many of my father's
paid servants have more food than they want, and here am I
dying of hunger! I will leave this place and go to my father and
say: Father, I have sinned against heaven and against you; I no
longer deserve to be called your son; treat me as one of your
paid servants.' So he left the place and went back to his father.

"While he was still a long way off, his father saw him and was
moved with pity. He ran to the boy, clasped him in his arms
and kissed him tenderly. Then his son said, 'Father, I have
sinned against heaven and against you. I no longer deserve
to be called your son.' But the father said to his servants,
'Quick! Bring out the best robe and put it on him; put a ring
on his finger and sandals on his feet. Bring the calf we have
been fattening, and kill it; we are going to have a feast,
a celebration, because this son of mine was dead and has
come back to life; he was lost and is found.' And they began
to celebrate.

*"Now the elder son was out in the fields, and on his way back,
as he drew near the house, he could hear music and dancing.
Calling one of the servants, he asked what it was all about.
'Your brother has come,' replied the servant, 'and your father
has killed the calf we had fattened because he has got him back
safe and sound.' He was angry then and refused to go in, and
his father came out to plead with him; but he answered his
father, 'Look, all these years I have slaved for you and never
once disobeyed your orders, yet you never offered me so much
as a kid for me to celebrate with my friends. But, for this son of
yours, when he comes back after swallowing up your property
— he and his women — you kill the calf we had been fattening.'*

*"The father said, 'My son, you are with me always and all I
have is yours. But it was only right we should celebrate and
rejoice, because your brother here was dead and has come to
life; he was lost and is found.' "*

COMMENTARY:

This is surely one of the most beautiful stories ever written!

It has been celebrated on stage, in art and music, and most significantly, it has been relived in countless lives and families.

Luke has so exquisitely rendered the feelings of the father and his sons that we are immediately drawn into the drama of this very human situation.

This is the story of a father who had two sons. He "lost them both, one in a foreign county, the other behind a barricade of self righteousness" (16, p. 182).

Popularly known as the Parable of the Prodigal Son, a more appropriate title might be the Parable of the Forgiving Father as the focus of the story is primarily on the Father's love and mercy toward his sons.

One can imagine the father's feelings when the younger son requested his inheritance, that is, what "would come" to him when his father died. Although it was not uncommon to see an estate divided among heirs before death, it seemed as if the younger son could not wait for his father to die.

As he watched his son go down the road, carrying "everything he had," the father must have been filled with apprehension for him.

His worst fears were realized! The son lavishly spent and wasted his father's gift until he was reduced to abject poverty. He was hungry; he was homeless; he was alone.

He had sunk to what, for a Jew, was the lowest possible level, for he was reduced to caring for the pigs of a Gentile landowner. For the Jews, the pig was considered to be the most "unclean" of all animals, and to be in the employ of a Gentile was to be under the influence and control of one who worshipped gods foreign to Yahweh.

Finally at the point of death — "I am dying of hunger" . . . "he came to his senses" and was filled with the desire to return home.

Even in the moment of deepest despair, his father's love was active in his memories. The father's deep longing for his son was present within the son's burning desire to return home. Though distant, father and son were united in love and yearning for each other — one calling, one responding.

The father received his son; he kissed him tenderly.

The son began his carefully-rehearsed admission of guilt. He said, "I have sinned against heaven and against you. I no longer deserve to be called your son."

He was interrupted by his father's uncontained joy. In the embrace of his father, the son was welcomed, forgiven and restored to full sonship. His father honored him with a fine robe to cover his nakedness. He received from his father a ring which signified the reinstatement of his authority as a son in his father's house. The sandals which were placed on his feet were further indication that he was not a slave, since only free people wore shoes.

The son had been lost and found. Now he knew what it meant to be his father's son. He was home!

The father was overjoyed, "My son has come to life; let the celebration begin!"

No sooner had the music and dancing begun than the father was angrily encountered by the other, older son.

However disappointed the father may have been by the older son's resentment and ill will, he had the wisdom not to take sides.

He may have sensed that the older son was suffering an alienation of his own. The older son's attitudes had distanced him from his brother to such an extent that he referred to him not as "my brother" but as "this son of yours." His self-righteous attitudes had prevented him from entering into a loving relationship not only with his brother but also with his father.

The elder son, too, was lost; he was lost in a foreign land of his own making.

The father responded as he had with his younger son. He was compassionate. He did not ridicule his son, but rebuked him gently, "You are with me always, and all that I have is yours."

All the father was able to do was invite the son to confront his negativity, accept his own position, and to enter into the joy of his brother's return.

As sons and daughters of our Father, we are being instructed through this story to confront whatever prejudicial and biased attitudes we may harbor against others.

We are invited to claim the reality of our inheritance as sons and daughters of a loving and merciful God.

The banquet is prepared. Will you enter into the joy of your Father?

SUGGESTED APPROACH TO PRAYER:

+ Daily prayer pattern, pages 1 and 2.
> I quiet myself and relax in the presence of God.
> I declare my dependency on God.

+ Grace: I ask for a deepening awareness of my sinfulness and a growing sorrow.

+ Method: Contemplation, page 3.
> I enter into this passage by allowing the story to enfold within me. I invite one of the sons to come forward. I assume his role and relive it in imagination, observing in detail his actions and words.

If I choose the younger son . . .
> I image as I request my inheritance, leave home, squander the money . . .

If I choose the elder son . . .
> I image my situation, my resentment toward my brother, the con-

versation with my father, his invitation . . .
Follow the story to its completion.

+ Closing: I close my prayer with a threefold conversation:

I turn to Mary who, with us, forms part of the community of all who have followed or do follow Christ. As mother of Jesus, she holds a special place in the communion of saints. In my own words, I ask her to obtain for me the gifts of:

— a deep knowledge of my sinfulness and a hatred for sin;
— an insight into the disorder in my life so that I may know how to refashion my life in the spirit of Jesus;
— an awareness of whatever may distract and separate me from him.

I turn to Jesus, begging him to ask the Father in His Name for these same gifts for me.

I turn to God the Father, that he who loved us so much that he sent his only Son will gift me with these same graces.

I pray the Our Father.

+ Review of Prayer:

I write in my journal any feeling, experiences or insights that surfaced during this period of prayer. I take special note of those which relate to my response to the Father.

Reread Luke 15:11-32 (p. 112).

COMMENTARY:

The story of the forgiving father and the two sons touches the center of each of us.

In a sense, we have within us, both sons. We are, at once, the younger pleasure-seeking son and the older, duty-bound, overly responsible son (62, p. 52). One of the two is dominant and most easily identifiable. The other, however, is nonetheless present and seeks to express himself also. Like an ignored child, the denied son reacts negatively, trying to get our attention.

If one identifies primarily with the elder, duty-bound son, his sinfulness will likely be an exaggeration of conscientiousness, concern for what others think, and a need to be accepted and approved. The denied pleasure-seeking son will likely make himself known by plunging the person into a "pout," whereby all joy will be absent, spontaneity squelched and sensitivity to others withheld.

On the other hand, if one identifies primarily with the younger pleasure-seeking son, his sinfulness will likely be in preoccupation with self and over-indulgence. The denied son will probably make himself known by subtly undermining the person's self esteem; as a consequence, the individual may become a slave to addictions and/or "binges" of compulsive rituals (e.g., food, drink, sex or spending).

The danger for us, as it was for the sons in the story, is an over-identification with either dimension. The moment we go "over the edge" with one we are catapulted into the negative side of the opposite (74, p. 34).

While it is important for us to recognize our preferred "son," the deeper challenge is to reconcile within ourselves both dimensions. Like the prodigal we need to "come to our senses"; that is, discover our true selves. That happens as we confront "our one-sidedness" (62, p. 119).

There is within us a wonderful potential, more than we could ever dream or imagine (Joel 3:1). We are invited to claim the gifts each son has to offer us. The elder son holds out for us the strength of stability, perseverance and faithfulness, while the younger son is offering us the joys of spontaneity, sensitivity and creativity.

We are called to come home to claim our gifts.

For us, as for the prodigal, to "come home" means to return to our Father. It is there, in the embrace of his love, that we are unconditionally accepted and our sins are forgiven. All that is fragmented within us is reconciled, and we experience new life.

> *God loved us with so much love that he was generous with His mercy: when we were dead through our sins, he brought us to life with Christ.*
>
> (Eph. 2:4-5a)

Our way to union, within ourselves and with God, is Jesus.
Paul's letter to the Ephesians reads like a commentary on this parable.

> *But now in Christ Jesus, you that used to be so far apart from us have been brought very close, by the blood of Christ. For he is the peace between us, and has made the two into one and broken down the barrier which used to keep them apart, actually destroying in his own person the hostility caused by the rules and decrees of the Law. This was to create one single New Man in himself out of the two of them and by restoring peace through the cross, to unite them both in a single Body and reconcile them with God. In his own person he killed the hostility. Later he came to bring the good news of peace, peace to you who were far away and peace to those who were near at hand. Through him, both of us have in the one Spirit our way to come to the Father. So you are no longer aliens or foreign visitors; you are citizens like all the saints, and part of God's household.*
>
> (Eph. 2:13-19)

SUGGESTED APPROACH TO PRAYER:

+ Daily prayer pattern, pages 1 and 2.
    I quiet myself and relax in the presence of God.
    I declare my dependency on God.

+ Grace: I ask for a deepening awareness of my sinfulness and a growing sorrow.

+ Method:

I meditatively reread Paul's letter to the Ephesians (2:4-5a, 13-19). I read it as a letter addressed personally to me. I respond by writing a letter to God, my Father.

I **thank God** for the gifts of each "son" that lives in me, what it is about each one that I love. . . .

I beg God to **help me**, by sending the living Spirit of Jesus to help me to reconcile and integrate these two wonderful, yet conflicting dimensions within myself. . . .

I **proclaim my love** for God, giving expression to my wish to accept fully all he intends for me, and to do what he requires to bring it to fullness. . . .

I **tell God that I am sorry** for the many times I have succumbed to the weakness and seductions of each dimension, thereby rejecting his love. I share with God the specific ways in which this has happened.

I close my letter by letting my heart speak of my deep desire to make his heart my home. I ask for the strength and wisdom of his love to protect me from moment to moment from every evil and temptation.

+ Closing: I close my prayer with a threefold conversation:

I turn to Mary who, with us, forms part of the community of all who have followed or do follow Christ. As mother of Jesus, she holds a special place in the communion of saints. In my own words, I ask her to obtain for me the gifts of:

— deep knowledge of my sinfulness and a hatred for sin;

— an insight into the disorder in my life so that I may know how to refashion my life in the spirit of Jesus;

— an awareness of whatever may distract and separate me from Christ, so that I may let go of all that deflects me from him.

I turn to Jesus, begging him to ask the Father in His Name for these same gifts for me.

I turn to God the Father, that he who loved us so much that he sent his only Son will gift me with these same graces.

I pray the Our Father.

+ Review of Prayer:

       I write in my journal the most prominent feelings I experienced while writing the letter to God.

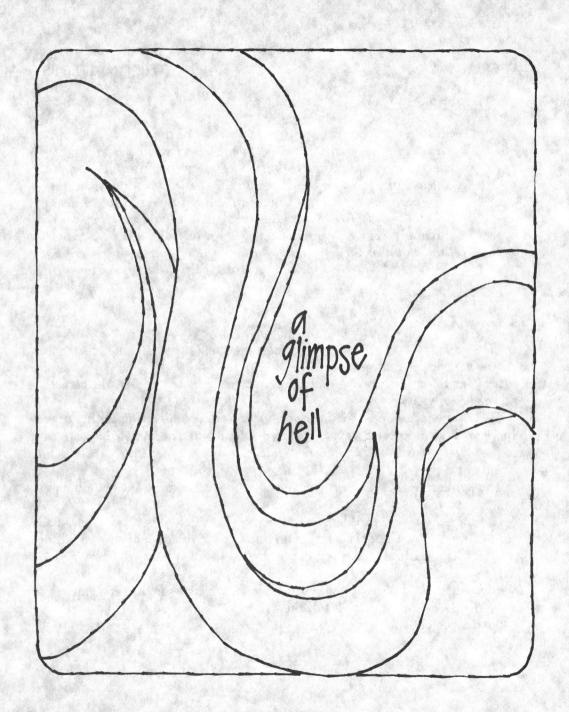

HEBREWS 10:26-29

If, after we have been given knowledge of the truth, we should deliberately commit any sins, then there is no longer any sacrifice for them. There will be left only the dreadful prospect of judgment and of the raging fire that is to burn rebels. Anyone who disregards the Law of Moses is ruthlessly put to death on the word of two witnesses or three; and you may be sure that anyone who tramples on the Son of God, and who treats the blood of the covenant which sanctified him as if it were not holy, and who insults the Spirit of grace, will be condemned to a far severer punishment.

COMMENTARY:

"The greater the knowledge, the greater the sin" (4, p. 124); the greater the sin, the greater the punishment.

It is one thing to sin when one is ignorant; it is quite another, deliberately and maliciously to choose to sin.

The "knowledge" that the author of Hebrews is addressing is the inner, experiential, heart knowledge that we have of Jesus. It is the knowledge that was received by those who had been called, initiated and baptized into the Christian community.

The writer is horrified at the thought that those who know Jesus could reject him.

How could one who had been freed from the burden of guilt, one who had received the gift of the Spirit, one who had been instructed by the words of Jesus, and enjoyed the fellowship of communion, possibly reject Christ?

How could that one "trample" such love underfoot? How could such a one treat and dismiss as nothing the death through which Jesus offered fullness of life? How could such a one "insult the Spirit"?

Such a person would be like a field that had been watered and blessed with good crops, and then later grew only brambles and thistles. It will end by being . . . abandoned . . . cursed . . . by being burnt (cf. Heb 6:8).

The greater the sin, the greater the punishment.

The price to be paid for the deliberate and absolute rejection of God's love defies imagination. In this passage it is described as a "raging fire that is to burn rebels."

Upon reading these words, medieval depictions of hell come to mind. In turn, these call up archetypal images of sinners writhing in pain, of putrid smells of sulphur and smoke, of isolation, and of unending darkness.

This common conception of hell was originally drawn from numerous biblical references to judgment and punishment.

In the Old Testament, though the word "hell" was not used, Gehenna, the Valley of Death, was designated as the place where the dead bodies of those who rebelled against Yahweh would lie. Referring to it, Isaiah said,

> And on their way out they will see the corpses of men
> who have rebelled against me.
> Their worm will not die nor their fire go out;
> they will be loathsome to all mankind. (66:24)

In the New Testament, Gehenna, the place of punishment, was described as the place where the wicked, body and soul, are destroyed (Mt 10:28). It was "a fiery lake of burning sulphur" (Rev 19:20) where those punished are salted with fire (Mk 9:49), and the "torture will not stop, day or night" (Rev 20:10). It is the domain of darkness and misery, of "weeping and grinding of teeth" (Mt 8:12). It is separated from this life by a "great gulf" (Lk 16:26).

In using these images in his teaching and parables, Jesus attempted to convey to his followers the seriousness of sin and its tragic consequences.

These strong and vivid images are meant to stimulate and elicit, by way of imagination, a totally human and integrated response of senses and intellect.

When Jesus spoke of hell as a domain of darkness, one could relate to that reality of hell by imaging a person who was in total darkness and thereby deprived of all light, both physical and intellectual. She/he would be terrified, groping and confused. In the imaging of the darkness, one's senses would take on an extraordinary acuteness, e.g., the intense quiet might be experienced as thunderous; the smell as musty; the taste like that of green fungus and the feel as that of a clammy mist.

As a result of this cumulative sense experience, the horror of hell would fill one with utter abhorrence, fear and repulsion at the prospect of such an eventuality for oneself.

However vivid the imaginative experience of hell, it would be merely a shadow of its devastating reality.

For, as McBrien points out, hell is not a place, nor even a state of being, but a "condition of non-being" (45, p. 1152).

Everything is at stake; all of who we are and all of who God intends us to be! Our total integrity rests on our moment-to-moment choosing. The choice is for or against God. To reject God totally, that is, to choose sin and to allow that sin to be lived in its entirety, would be to lose everything. We would be totally alienated, not only from God but from our very selves. We would no longer "be."

While neither Jesus nor the church ever taught that any one is actually in hell, we do carry in our human frailty the seeds of such destruction. The realization of this possibility can only cause one to fear, to have a "chaste fear" (59, p. 96) of ourselves and our capability for evil.

SUGGESTED APPROACH TO PRAYER:

+ Daily prayer pattern, pages 1 and 2.
> I quiet myself and relax in the presence of God.
> I declare my dependency on God.

+ Grace: I ask for a sense of the loss that is the essence of hell so that in the event that I lose the vision of God's love, the fear of hell would keep me from sin.

+ Method:
> In imagination, I enter into the experience of hell. I let myself become aware of the absolute finality, confinement and shallowness of hell as opposed to the length, breadth, height and depth of Christ's love.

> Using the New Testament images quoted in the commentary on

page 124 I will further enter into the experience of hell with my whole being, using in turn each of my five senses:

seeing the fires

hearing the wailing and grinding of teeth

smelling the smoke and sulphur

tasting the bitterness

touching the burning coals.

+ Closing:

"Once I have let the awfulness of this experience sink deep within me, I begin to talk to Christ our Lord about it. I talk to him about all the people who have lived — the many who lived before his coming and who deliberately closed in upon themselves and chose such a hell for all eternity, the many who walked with him in his own country and who rejected his call to love, the many who still keep rejecting the call to love and remain locked in their own chosen hell.

I give thanks to Jesus that he has not put an end to my life and allowed me to fall into any of these groups. All I can do is to give thanks to him that up to this very moment he has shown himself so loving and merciful to me. Then I close with an Our Father" (28, p. 47).

+ Review of Prayer:

I will write in my journal the "vision" of hell which I experienced in my imagination. I will write the feelings that most gripped me.

Reread Hebrews 10:26-29 and its commentary on pages 124-126.

SUGGESTED APPROACH TO PRAYER:

+ Daily prayer pattern, pages 1 and 2.
    I quiet myself and relax in the presence of God.
    I declare my dependency on God.
+ Grace: I ask for a sense of the loss that is the essence of hell so that in the event that I would lose the vision of God's love, the fear of hell would keep me from sin.
+ Method:
    In my imagination, I enter into the experience of hell. I become aware of one of my most basic disorders, that is, the area in which I am most prone to sin.

    I consider how I have succumbed to this sin in the past. I allow myself to imagine what would happen if I were to give free and complete reign to that sin. I imagine in detail all its ramifications: its effects on those I love, on the community I live in, on myself. . . .

    Using each of my five senses, I will further enter into the hell I would cause by this sin.
    I will see it.
    I will hear it.
    I will smell it.
    I will taste it.
    I will touch it.
    I will let the seriousness, the pain and the sorrow for my sinfulness enter deeply within me.
+ Closing:
    "Once I have let the awfulness of this experience sink deep within me, I begin to talk to Christ our Lord about it. I talk to him about all the people who have lived — the many who lived before his coming and who deliberately

closed in upon themselves and chose such a hell for all eternity, the many who walked with him in his own country and who rejected his call to love, the many who still keep rejecting the call to love and remain locked in their own chosen hell.

I give thanks to Jesus that he has not put an end to my life and allowed me to fall into any of these groups. All I can do is to give thanks to him that up to this very moment he has shown himself so loving and merciful to me. Then I close with an Our Father" (28, p. 47).

+ Review of Prayer:

I write in my journal the sorrow I experienced for my sinfulness.

REVELATIONS 18:2, 21-23a

*"Babylon has fallen, Babylon the Great has fallen, and has
become the haunt of devils and a lodging for every foul spirit
and dirty, loathsome bird."*

. . . .

*Then a powerful angel picked up a boulder like a great mill-
stone, and as he hurled it into the sea, he said, "That is how
the great city of Babylon is going to be hurled down, never
to be seen again.*

> *"Never again in you, Babylon,*
> *will be heard the song of harpists and minstrels,*
> *the music of flute and trumpet;*
> *never again will craftsmen of every skill be found*
> *or the sound of the mill be heard;*
> *never again will shine the light of the lamp,*
> *never again will be heard*
> *the voices of bridegroom and bride."*

COMMENTARY:

There once was a small band of people who lived together harmoniously.
The people individually and together had a vision and a task: to create. So
powerful was the vision that it was as if they had been mysteriously chosen.

Together they built a small city and in the center constructed a beautiful
temple in which to worship the God of their joy. The light that burned in the
sanctuary could be seen from every home in the city.

Gregarious and fun-loving, the people took advantage of every possible
occasion to celebrate. They loved to sing and to dance. Weddings were three-
day affairs.

Every day they went eagerly to their task of creating and were extraordinarily successful.

Not only were their creations appreciated and sought throughout the known world, but their style of community was emulated by many in the hopes that they, too, might experience the release of such creative power.

As the years went by, the reputation and fame of the community grew. More and more people came to purchase their works of art.

As the orders began to accumulate, the artists experienced pressure from having to produce so much. No longer did they welcome each new day. By nightfall, they were too tired to pray or to enjoy each other.

The people began to be preoccupied with the money from the escalating sales of their art. The money grew to such proportions that, finding no place large enough in which to store and guard it, they built a bank at each corner of the city. These buildings rose like four giant pillars.

In their new-found fame and affluence, the people became very possessive of their unique gift of creativity. They were unwilling to share the secrets of their craft, even among themselves. They rationalized that the power of creativity might be dissipated through sharing.

Filled with fear, they created an army, and prepared themselves for an imagined attack from those who might covet their riches.

No longer trustful, the people began to do things that they would not originally have considered. They constructed a wall with gates that were kept locked even during daylight. Though they had telephones, they were not connected with the outside world. Visitors from the outside became progressively rarer and not welcome. Of those few who chose to leave, stories circulated that they had met their death beyond the gates.

Something was happening to the people, and it became ever more obvious. The rooms in which the people had created changed from centers of exhilaration to places of tomblike silence. Creations were turned out one after another, but each one looked exactly like the preceding one.

If perchance someone with bright eyes laughingly produced a new design, it was quickly squelched as a deformation. There was no freshness, no vitality; the power was gone.

Slowly through the years the community grew increasingly isolated from the outside and divided within. Chaos had come (Is 34:11). Marriages were few and always without festivity (Jer 7:34). Births were infrequent. The spirit of the people had died. The light in the temple had long since flickered out (Jer 25:10). The building itself was in shambles (Ez 26:12) and had become a shelter for mice and for owls (Is 34:11).

Years later people remembered the community, and went into the wilderness in search for it. They looked in vain (Ez 26:21).

+   +   +   +

The story illustrates the spiritual collapse of an entire community of people. Their withdrawal, self-preoccupation and mistrust of others resulted in the loss of creativity, joy and spirit. Within the hell of their own making, they ceased to be.

In the book of Revelations, we find a discription of the collapse of the city of Babylon. Because Revelations was addressed to the Christian community during a time of persecution, it is filled with symbolic images that would have been understandable only to the initiated members.

On one level of meaning, Babylon signified Rome whose emperor ruled the known world. As the capital of the ancient land of Jewish exile, Babylon came to be identified with all that was opposed to Yahweh. She was thought of as an evil, immoral city. Her collapse and fall was seen by the Hebrew prophets as a sign of God's judgment and punishment.

The depths of her collapse was equaled only by the height of her former accomplishments and creativity. Even today, Babylon is synonymous with art and architecture. The wanton deterioration of this once beautiul and prominent center of culture was tragic.

In its glory, Babylon had a highly developed and humane system of government. The Babylonians were responsible for making significant advances in the areas of science, astrology and mathematics. Artifacts from that period give evidence of a highly skilled craftsmanship.

One of the most valuable contributions of the Babylonians to modern civilization was that they committed to writing the myths, hymns and history of their times. These songs and stories provide a link between Babylon and early Judaic traditions and beliefs. These literary treasures have made a significant impact on our contemporary understanding of scripture and its historical rootedness.

Ironically, the very gifts that brought the Babylonians to such an extraordinary level of civilization influenced its downfall.

In spite of the idealism expressed in some of its hymns and other writings, its religion had little moral impact. Emphasizing this world and its goods, it was an undemanding and superficial religion which was conducive to superstitious practices.

For the prophets of Judah, the fall of Babylon was never simply a matter of external political and economic forces; it was the logical consequences of a people materially unrestrained, morally undisciplined and religiously sterile.

Babylon, that pearl of kingdoms, the jewel and boast of Chaldeans,
like Sodom and Gomorrah shall be overthrown by God.
Never more will anyone live there or be born there
from generation to generation.
No Arab will pitch his tent there, nor shepherds feed their flocks,
But beasts of the desert will lie there, and owls fill its houses.

(Is 13:19-20, cf. Jer 50:1,45; 51:55)

The Book of Revelations draws on the prophets in its bitter criticism of the sinfulness of the Roman Empire. The judgment of such sinfulness is described in words that plunge deeply into our human consciousness and cause a response of repulsion and fear.

That response is none other than that which we experience when, in our more lucid moments, we contemplate our world in **its** sinfulness and **our** personal share in it.

SUGGESTED APPROACH TO PRAYER:

+ Daily prayer pattern, pages 1 and 2.
    I quiet myself and relax in the presence of God.

133

I declare my dependency on God.

+ Grace: I ask for a sense of the loss that is the essence of hell so that in the event that I would lose the vision of God's love, the fear of hell would keep me from sin.

+ Method:

As I enter this time of prayer, I become aware of the pain of loss that accompanies all sin, and the incredible sin that inflicts our planet.

I will take into my hands a real or imagined globe of the earth. Turning it gently and slowly in my hands, I will bring to mind and heart all the sins of the people of the earth.

I will consider:

. . . the greediness and over-consumption, which has created widespread poverty, starvation, and scarcities . . .

. . . the violence that has resulted in rape, and abuse, and murders . . .

. . . the irreverence that has torn families apart, split churches and ruined government officials . . . polluted our air and water. . . .

I will continue in this manner to consider the horror of the sins that encircle our globe.

Using each of my senses in turn, I will try to grasp the gravity of this reality. I will taste . . . see . . . hear . . . feel . . . smell the sin.

+ Closing:

I speak to Christ of whatever surfaces in my mind and heart. I thank him that, in spite of the sinfulness of the world and my share in it, he continues in his mercy to preserve the earth from total destruction.

I close with an Our Father.

+ Review of Prayer:

I write in my journal whatever feelings, e.g., grief and sense of loss, I experienced in this prayer period.

the call of Christ and our response

"Receive the Holy Spirit. For those whose sins you forgive, they are forgiven; for those whose sins you retain, they are retained."

(Jn 20:22-23)

This was the Easter greeting of Jesus to his gathered and frightened disciples on the day of his resurrection. He came, bringing them the gift of forgiveness.

We must not underestimate the gift. The pagan world knew nothing of forgiveness — only fate. The good news of the Old Testament was that **God forgave**, and that through faith in new beginnings, God acted in the brokenness of his people. In the New Testament, **Jesus** himself **forgave** and, in doing so, bore the criticism and the accusation of blasphemy that brought him to his death.

Yet, his first words to his disciples is to share with them the incredible good news that the Spirit of God's own forgiving love dwells within us, and that the power to be forgiven and to forgive has been entrusted to us.

Forgiveness awaits us in the heart and hands of the Risen Jesus, in the hearts and hands of our fellow Christians. Jesus' words to the disciples invite us to bring the burden of our sinfulness, our brokenness, our need for forgiveness to another. "Confess your sins to one another" (James 5:16). For many Christians, this will be a pastor, i.e., an ordained minister who is pledged to confidentiality. For those who do not have this as part of their religious tradition, that "other" may be a friend or confidante, some wise man or woman who knows how to listen, and how to hear.

After the past weeks of praying about the roots and effects of our sinfulness and God's merciful love for us, it can be a deepening of the healing to make a "confession," that is, to share with another one's need for healing and forgiveness.

The following is a preparation for that confession:

1. THANKS — What has Christ done for me? What am I trying to do? How through Christ's help, did I succeed? What signs of God's love (people, events) have I experienced in my recent past? Why did things go well

(rested, less tension, more prayer, positive focus, etc.)?

2. EXAMINATION — Look at the cross and ask, "What have I done for Christ? What am I trying to do? How does Christ want me further healed? What were the low points — times of tension, discouragement, boredom, hurt, etc.?

Responses to hurt:

Pride — When did I fail to see my true worth and so have to [put on a mask] for others, or lie, judge, fail to listen, be opinionated or touchy, ignore the successes of others?

[What does my critical judging of others say about my own sinfulness? Am I "puffed up"?]

Covetousness — When do I act as if money, [possessions], time are mine, rather than a gift?

Lust — How is each part of my body not used to love others?

Anger — What do I fear? Worry about? Resent in others? Find hard to forgive? Have I grown from the failures, tensions, hurts?

When did I react rather than act, e.g., compete, conform?

When do I avoid difficult persons, e.g., egotists, complainers, the needy?

Do I face my anger rather than deny it and turn it on myself causing physical complaints like headaches, stomach problems, less laughter, etc.?

Gluttony — How do I escape insecurity? Too much drink, food, TV, study, work, [compulsive spending]?

Envy — Do I criticize others to build myself up? Am I bored when others are praised?

Do I belittle my success to hear others remind me of it?

Do I listen just to the words of others, or do I have empathy with their feelings?

Do I make new friends? Among difficult people? Am I faithful to friends? To God?

[Laziness] — Do I fail to take risks and make sacrifices because I want a tension-free life?

Where do I fall into routines rather than live with [enthusiasm]?

Do I learn from the past, live in the present, and plan for the future?

Do I take time to improve myself spiritually, mentally and physically?

What good do I omit doing (corporal and spiritual works)?

How do I ignore building up my family, community, church, those I meet?

What parts of my day would Christ live differently?

3. SORROW — How did it hurt Christ in me or in others?

Which of the above bothers me the most? How does it hurt Christ in me? In others? How has it spread? Am I sorry just because it hurt me and others or because it hurt Christ too? Am I sorry to the point where I want to change, even at great effort?

4. HEALING — Why am I doing it to Christ?

Am I feeling or covering any insecurity, guilt, fear, tension, failure or hostility? Why am I attracted to this action? What do I gain from it, e.g., power, popularity, etc.? How could I have been hurt that would lead me to respond in that way? Is there any pattern to it? When did it begin? Can I give this all to Christ?

5. FORGIVING — Can I forgive as Christ forgives?

How has Christ forgiven me (unconditionally, readily, totally)? Can I extend his forgiveness to those who hurt me? Can I see how they were reacting to other hurts or my actions and not just to me? Have I forgiven them to the point of seeing some good that came from it, e.g., empathy toward those hurt, trying harder, more trust in Christ? Do I feel toward them as Christ would? Can I say what Christ would say?

6. CHANGING — What will I do for Christ?

Do I really believe I can be closer to Christ than ever before? Do I feel like the prodigal son (Lk 15), or the woman who washed Jesus' feet (Lk 7:36ff)? How would Christ live my life? Can I imagine myself doing the same? Why do I want to change?

How can I remind myself to change, e.g., [the exercise of the will, (p. 90)], daily self denial, or a prayer, or a reward? Can I suggest a

140

penance, e.g., write a letter, make a visit, give a compliment, [fast], etc.?

(Preparation drawn principally, with some modification, and with permission, from HEALING OF MEMORIES, pp. 89-91, 132) Reprinted from HEALING OF MEMORIES by Dennis Linn and Matthew Linn. ©1974 by The Missionary Society of St. Paul the Apostle in the State of New York. Used by permission of the Paulist Press.

LUKE 7:36-50

One of the Pharisees invited him to a meal. When he arrived at the Pharisee's house and took his place at table, a woman came in who had a bad name in the town. She had heard he was dining with the Pharisee and had brought with her an alabaster jar of ointment. She waited behind him at his feet, weeping, and her tears fell on his feet, and she wiped them away with her hair; then she covered his feet with kisses and anointed them with the ointment.

When the Pharisee who had invited him saw this, he said to himself, "If this man were a prophet, he would know who this woman is that is touching him and what a bad name she has." Then Jesus took him up and said, "Simon, I have something to say to you." "Speak, Master," was the reply. "There was once a creditor who had two men in his debt; one owed him five hundred denarii, the other fifty. They were unable to pay, so he pardoned them both. Which of them will love him more?" "The one who was pardoned more, I suppose," answered Simon. Jesus said, "You are right."

Then he turned to the woman. "Simon," he said, "you see this woman? I came into your house, and you poured no water over my feet, but she has poured out her tears over my feet and wiped them away with her hair. You gave me no kiss, but she has been covering my feet with kisses ever since I came in. You did not anoint my head with oil, but she has anointed my feet with ointment. For this reason I tell you that her sins, her many sins, must have been forgiven her, or she would not have shown such great love. It is the [one] who is forgiven little who shows little love." Then he said to her, "Your sins are forgiven."

Those who were with him at table began to say to themselves, "Who is this man, that he even forgives sins?" But he said to the woman, "Your faith has saved you; go in peace."

COMMENTARY:

"Go in peace!"

Shalom — this was the Easter greeting of Jesus (Jn 20:21).

This term, coming to us from the Old Testament, expresses much more than our English word "peace." It is a wish to someone for their total completeness and well being, in which nothing is lacking.

This peace is a favored theme in the writings of Luke.

In the beautiful story of the woman who washed and anointed the feet of Jesus, St. Luke reveals to us the way to Shalom. He shows this peace as the fruit of the faith, forgiveness and love of the woman. In this narration, Luke included a parable of two debtors which serves to interpret the event.

The woman is identified as a "sinner" (RSV). In Aramaic, the language of New Testament times, the word used for "sinner" was "debtor." Thus the parable provides the connecting link between the event and the teaching of Jesus.

The scene opened at the home of a Pharisee. Guests had gathered in the open courtyard where a meal was about to be served. As was the custom, the guests were not seated but reclined on couches near the table.

Jesus was there, having been invited by Simon, a Pharisee. Luke does not tell why Simon invited Jesus. Perhaps he was one of the Pharisees who sincerely admired Jesus, or he may have sought to impress his other guests with the presence of the popular itinerant rabbi. There is also the possibility that he wanted to provoke Jesus into an argument.

It was not unusual when there was a visiting rabbi for uninvited guests to come and listen to the conversation.

During the meal, from among the onlookers, a woman came forward. She had come deliberately to see Jesus and went directly to the foot of his couch where she "waited behind him at his feet."

As she stood there, she began to weep. When her tears fell unintentionally on his feet, she bent over and wiped them with her hair.

Overwhelmed at the touch of that moment, she kissed his feet. She reached for the small vial of perfume that she, like other Jewish women, wore around her neck. Kneeling, she broke open the alabaster jar and proceeded to pour it on his feet, anointing them with its aromatic oil.

Who was this woman? Luke does not tell us precisely. We know only that she had a "bad reputation," that she was a "sinner." Although it has been commonly assumed that she was a prostitute, some scholars suggest that she may have been the wife of an outcast, e.g., perhaps a despised publican (14, p. 138).

Simon's inner response to the woman's telling actions was one of irritation. Jesus may have perceived a flash of doubt or skepticism in Simon's eyes.

Jesus spoke, "Simon, I have something to say to you."

He began to relate the story of the two debtors who were freed of their indebtedness. Then, Jesus posed a question which forced Simon to admit reluctantly the fundamental truth that the more one is pardoned, the more grateful one is.

Jesus pressed Simon further. He demonstrated to Simon how an experience of being unconditionally forgiven can motivate a person to human acts of extraordinary love and generosity. Jesus took Simon's answer to his question at the conclusion of the parable and made a direct application to Simon himself.

He drew a harsh comparison between Simon and the woman.

Simon had neglected even the most elemental Jewish/Eastern forms of etiquette. One absolutely never welcomed an invited guest without offering the courtesies of hospitality which included washing the dust from the traveler's feet, embracing the guest with a kiss, and anointing his head with oil.

These outward functional acts had deep psychic roots. For a desert people, water was life, and the kiss was a sign of friendship and forgiveness. Perfumed oil was symbolic of healing and joy. Taken together, these beautiful symbolic acts formed a greeting and an experience of Shalom for all who entered as guest.

Simon had seriously dishonored his guest and his position as host.

On the other hand, the woman came freely and courageously to see Jesus. In his presence her inner gratitude and love for Him found expression in the tears that flowed from the deep sources of life and joy within her. Oblivious to those around her, she spontaneously began to kiss the feet of Jesus repeatedly. Her love spilled over as she poured her fragrant oil on his feet.

Jesus called Simon to recognize that such a free and total expression of love could only arise from a heart forgiven and overwhelmed with thankfulness.

Poor Simon! If he showed little love, it was because he had never known the depth of his own thirst and need to be forgiven. To the woman, Jesus said, "Go in peace, your faith has saved you." Who is this man, that he even forgives sins?

SUGGESTED APPROACH TO PRAYER:

+ Daily prayer pattern, pages 1 and 2.

I quiet myself and relax in the presence of God.

I declare my dependency on God.

+ Grace: I ask Christ our Lord that I may hear his call and be ready and willing to respond with total generosity to his will and intent for me.

+ Method: Contemplation. p. 3.

I image myself as having received the fullness of forgiveness from Christ.

I place myself in the role of the woman and go to the house of the Pharisee.

Using all my senses, I place myself in the situation. I approach Jesus, allowing whatever tears may flow to wash over his feet. I anoint his feet. I look at the face of Jesus and take within myself his expression of compassion and love. I listen to and receive his consoling words to me.

+ Closing:

I close my prayer with a conversation with Christ, expressing to him my gratitude and love. I let my heart speak in total openness and offering. With him I pray the Our Father.

+ Review of Prayer:

I write in my journal any feelings, experiences or insights I received during this prayer period.

THE PRAYER OF THE CALL OF
CHRIST AND OUR RESPONSE

Preparation: I begin my prayer by placing myself in the presence of God.
Aware of my dependence on him, I beg him to direct every-
thing in me — all I think, do and say — **more and more** to his praise and
service.

I ask for the grace that I may hear his call and be ready and
willing to respond with total generosity to his will and intent for me.

Part I: In this first part of my prayer, I will bring to mind some women
and men who, by their inspiring lives, have won the admiration of
countless others. I consider how they have magnetically drawn people to share
in their vision, and in some instances, to join them in their work. I consider in
some depth the life of a great man or woman. The following list is merely offered
as suggestions. Choose one man or woman whom you admire — John XXIII,
Coretta King, Martin Luther, Dag Hammersjold, Teresa of Avila, Mother Teresa
of Calcutta, Mahatma Ghandi, Winston Churchill, Francis of Assisi, Chief Joseph,
Albert Schweitzer, Madam Curie. . . .

As I bring this person to mind, I will reflect on:
+ how people have responded to him / her, been inspired and followed
  the vision and / or joined this person in his / her lifestyle, struggle,
  pain, and work;
+ the price this person paid, i.e., all he / she may have given up . . .
  material possessions, family and home, friends, reputation, life
  itself.

Part II: In the second part of my prayer I see before me, Christ, our Lord.
I prayerfully read the following quotations (72, p. 88) considering
how Jesus is leader and king.

*. . . He has taken us out of the power of darkness and created
a place for us in the kingdom of the Son that he loves, and in
him, we gain our freedom, the forgiveness of our sins. He is the
image of the unseen God and the first-born of all creation, for*

146

*in him were created all things in heaven and on earth . . . and
he holds all things in unity.*

(Colossians 1:13-16a,17b)

*Through him the Father wants to gather a people to himself from
age to age so that from east to west a perfect offering may be
made to the glory of His Name.*

(Eucharistic Prayer III)

*You anointed your only-begotten Son, our Lord Jesus Christ,
eternal priest and king of the universe . . . that he should . . .
deliver to your divine majesty an everlasting kingdom of truth
and life, a kingdom of holiness and grace, a kingdom of justice,
love and peace.*

(Preface from the Liturgy of Christ the King)

I consider: the words of Jesus, our leader, as he says, in effect, It is my desire
to enter into the glory of my Father and to gather the entire world,
in unity, to share in this same glory. It is my desire to overcome any evil
obstacle that is contrary to that goal. If you wish to join me, you must be willing
to choose to labor with me . . . to do all that is required, whatever pain or
sacrifice is needed so that together we will enter the fullness of life, the glory of
God, my Father.

I consider: how, even though Christ is calling the entire world, he is in a
particular way calling me to respond and to accept my unique role
in the achievement of this goal — the Kingdom of God.

I consider: how reasonable and sensible this goal is, and how Jesus has assured
me of its success. Taking all this into consideration, how can I
possibly refuse to join him?

Finally, I consider: how people who have totally responded to the call of
Jesus have not only offered all they were and had, but
have withdrawn from and fought against anything that was a hindrance or
distraction to their commitment to him.

147

+ Closing. I will consider: what I desire my response and offering to him to be. I speak to Christ of this. I will close with an Our Father.

+ Review of Prayer:

I will write in my journal how I am experiencing Christ's care and my response.

PHIL 3:7-10

> *But because of Christ, I have come to consider all these advantages that I had as disadvantages. Not only that, but I believe nothing can happen that will outweigh the supreme advantage of knowing Christ Jesus my Lord. For him I have accepted the loss of everything, and I look on everything as so much rubbish if only I can have Christ and be given a place in him. I am no longer trying for perfection by my own efforts, the perfection that comes from the Law, but I want only the perfection that comes through faith in Christ, and is from God and based on faith. All I want is to know Christ and the power of his resurrection and to share his sufferings by reproducing the pattern of his death.*

COMMENTARY:

On the Road to Damascus, Paul passed from death to life (Acts 9:1-19; 22:5-16; 26:10-18).

Paul's conversion was dramatic, a profound rebirth. From that day he courageously drew on his own transforming experience to inspire others to risk their own passage from darkness to light (Acts 26:17-18).

Paul's conversion was traumatic! At the very moment that his dreams, hopes and ambitions reached fulfillment, they collapsed.

In his blindness, Paul had chosen the wrong road.

Gifted and ambitious, Paul allowed the first half of his life to be dictated and controlled by his fanatic allegiance to the authoritarian pharisaic value system. This allegiance drove him to channel all his energies toward the development and projection of the perfect pharisaic ideal.

Externally, Paul appeared to be the embodiment of that ideal. Internally, he was sterile, having cut himself off from his own identity and creativity.

He had goaded himself (Acts 26:14) on through years of study until he attained the position of unchallengeable expertise in the law (Acts 22:3).

He had managed easily to win the approval of the high priests and elders.

Having done violence to himself, Paul set out in his misguided zeal to destroy the new Christian uprising.

Paul was undoubtedly headed in the wrong direction. However, "about mid-day a bright light from heaven suddenly shone around him" (Acts 22:6).

He heard a voice calling his name, "Saul, Saul, why are you persecuting me?" (Acts 22:7). This question initiated Paul's self-confrontation. Overwhelmed by the force and power of such great light, Paul was blinded for three days.

One can imagine the inner upheaval and disorganization that Paul must have experienced! It was as if his entire life had been turned upside down. His interior orientation was inundated with new perspectives, questions, and awareness which rendered his former mindset "rubbish." All his former advantages were now seen as disadvantages.

Weakened and unable to see, Paul was not left abandoned. A member of the Christian community was sent by God to minister to him.

Into his empty heart Paul received the Spirit of Jesus. With the strength and vision of his Risen Lord, Paul saw with new eyes.

After a lifetime of seeking God in the Law through the pursuit of his own perfection, Paul had met God in the human face of Jesus.

Nothing would ever be the same for Paul. His former self-righteousness and rigid adherence to rules and regulations had given way to an authentic, **right** relationship with God and a commitment to the needs of His people. The focus had shifted from Paul to Christ, from law to love, from an addiction to perfection toward a mature completeness. Blind obedience yielded to creative vision, intellectual knowledge to the intimate "knowing of the heart." The violent persecutor had become the persuasive teacher.

All Paul wanted now was to "know Christ and the power of his resurrection and to share his sufferings by reproducing the patterns of his death" (Phil. 3:10).

For Paul, faith could never again be simply an intellectual assent. His faith had become a relationship involving an inner sensitivity which put Paul in touch with the fundamental meaning and fullness of life. This extraordinary gift of faith found its expression in Paul's total commitment to Christ.

Through this "conviction and commitment" (31, 54), Paul received the power of the Resurrection, the Spirit of Jesus.

This spirit gave Paul the power to work untiringly in proclaiming the incredible wonder that awaited those who would believe.

> As kingfishers catch fire, dragonflies draw flame;
> . . .
> Each mortal thing does one thing and the same:
> . . . *myself* it speaks and spells;
> Crying What I do is me: for that I came.
> I say more: the just man justices;
> Keeps grace: that keeps all his goings graces;
> Acts in God's eye what in God's eye he is —
> Christ . . .

(11, p. 95)

For the rest of his life, he traveled the known world, suffering every inconvenience, to deliver the people from darkness to light (Acts 26:18).

APPROACH TO PRAYER:

I pray the prayer of THE CALL OF CHRIST AND MY RESPONSE, page 146, using St. Paul as the person in the first part.

I continue with the second part, Christ's personal call to me, concluding with the closing and review as outlined.

LUKE 5:1-11

Now he was standing one day by the Lake of Gennesaret, with the crowd pressing around him listening to the word of God, when he caught sight of two boats close to the bank. The fishermen had gone out of them and were washing their nets. He got into one of the boats — it was Simon's — and asked him to put out a little from the shore. Then he sat down and taught the crowds from the boat.

When he had finished speaking, he said to Simon, "Put out into deep water and pay out your nets for a catch." "Master," Simon replied, "we worked hard all night long and caught nothing, but if you say so, I will pay out the nets." And when they had done this they netted such a huge number of fish that their nets began to tear, so they signaled to their companions in the other boat to come and help them; when these came, they filled the two boats to sinking point.

When Simon Peter saw this he fell at the knees of Jesus saying, "Leave me, Lord; I am a sinful man." For he and all his companions were completely overcome by the catch they had made; so also were James and John, sons of Zebedee, who were Simon's partners. But Jesus said to Simon, "Do not be afraid; from now on it is men you will catch." Then, bringing their boats back to land, they left everything and followed him.

COMMENTARY:

This is a story about a miracle, the miracle of a marvelous catch of fish, and the wonder of Peter who heard the voice of Jesus and "left everything and followed him."

What could be more wonderful than a beautiful catch of fish, especially after a long, hard night of unsuccessful fishing?

Luke tells us about this miraculous catch of fish in order to stir our admiration for Christ and to call forth our belief in Him and the treasures he promised us.

Fishing was a way of life for the people who lived along the shores of Gennesaret. Their lives revolved around the daily task of the necessity of catching fish. It was the mainstay of their diet, and fishing was their principal occupation. Fishing was hard work and frequently dangerous, as sudden storms were not uncommon to the lake. Great pride was taken in being an able fisherman, and the skill was handed on from father to son.

What could possibly have been more wonderful for **these** people than to bring home a great catch?

In the New Testament there are many stories involving fish. One of the most beautiful is the story of how Jesus multiplied and fed bread and fish to the people who were hungry after having spent a day with Him in the desert.

Among the stories told of Jesus' appearances after he rose from the dead, is the delightful one in which he ate some fish to show his disciples that he was truly alive (Lk 24:42-43). On another occasion, he surprised his disciples by preparing breakfast for them when they came ashore after a night of fishing. Jesus was there and "they saw . . . a charcoal fire with fish cooking on it." Jesus invited them to bring some of their own fish (Jn 21:9-13).

It follows that, for the early Christians, fish took on a significance beyond its primary importance as daily food. Christ Himself came to be symbolized by the fish.

In the underground remains of the catacombs of Rome, one can still see the outlines of fish with the Greek acronym for fish — IXΘYC — superimposed upon it. The letters correspond with the initial Greek letter of each word in the phrase, "Jesus Christ God's Son Saves."

Long before the time of Jesus, fish held a religious significance. Babylonian writings from the third century B.C. record a myth of Oannes, a fish god, who emerged from the sea to teach men and women the arts and the crafts of civilization (46, p. 279).

The symbolism of the fish is deeply rooted in our evolutionary, collective human history. Dreams continue to reflect the symbolism of the fish as the untapped energy and limitless possibilities of the subconscious (62, p. 99).

These living streams of Revelation, mythology, history and dreams flow and merge so that we, today, see in the numinous quality of the fish, the symbol of the totality of the Risen Christ, whose power, when tapped, can release in us an energy, creativity and possibilities of miraculous proportion.

This was the promise Christ held out to Peter when he said, "Put out into the deep water and pay out your nets for a catch."

A simple, down-to-earth man, Peter had been fishing all his life. Now, at the sight of such a catch, and in the presence and power of Jesus, Peter was overwhelmed.

He recognized Jesus as Lord!

Falling on his knees, he confessed his sinfulness. "Leave me, Lord, I am a sinful man."

Jesus reassured him, "Don't be afraid" . . . In companionship with me, "it is men you will catch."

In the power of the word that yielded the miraculous draught of fish, Peter became, in solidarity with Christ, the magnetic lure that would gather many into the kingdom.

Peter continued to be overwhelmed. The power and promise of Christ had gripped him with such force that from that day on, Peter committed and conformed his life to patterning that of Christ. The heart of Peter became the heart of Christ.

He left everything and followed Jesus.

APPROACH TO PRAYER:

I pray the prayer of THE CALL OF CHRIST AND MY RESPONSE, page 146, using St. Peter as the person in Part I. I continue with the second part, Christ's personal call to me, concluding with the closing and review as outlined.

I use the prayer, THE CALL OF CHRIST AND MY RESPONSE, page 146. I particularly concentrate on Part II. I will write a personal prayer of offering to Jesus. During the coming weeks, I will frequently use this prayer.

Appendices

FOR SPIRITUAL DIRECTORS:

The passages and commentaries are keyed to the Spiritual Exercises of St. Ignatius. The number in parentheses indicates the numbered paragraph as found in the original text.

INDEX OF SCRIPTURE PASSAGES

* Page numbers preceded by a bold "L" are in *Love: A Guide for Prayer*, Take and Receive series.

BIBLIOGRAPHY

1. Abbot, Walter M., ed. *The Documents of Vatican II*. New York: American Press, 1966.
2. Albright, W. F., and C. S. Mann. *Matthew*. Garden City, NY: Doubleday & Co., 1971.
3. Anderson, Bernard W. *Understanding the Old Testament*. Englewood Cliffs, NJ: Prentice-Hall, Inc., 1975.
4. Barclay, William. *The Daily Study Bible Series*. Philadelphia: The Westminster Press, 1975.
5. Barth, Karl. *A Shorter Commentary on Romans*. Richmond: John Knox Press, 1963.
6. Barth, Markus. *Ephesians 1-3*. Garden City, NY: Doubleday & Co., Inc., 1974.
7. Bergant, Diane. *Job, Ecclesiastes*. Wilmington, DE: Michael Glazier, Inc., 1982.
8. Blenkinsopp, Joseph. *From Adam to Abraham*. Glen Rock, NJ: Paulist Press, 1966.
9. Boadt, Lawrence. *Jeremiah 1-25*. Wilmington, DE: Michael Glazier, Inc., 1982.
10. Boucher, Madeleine I. *The Parables*. Wilmington, DE: Michael Glazier, Inc., 1981.
11. Bridges, Robert, ed. *Poems of Gerard Manley Hopkins*. New York: Oxford University Press, 1948.
12. Bright, John. *Jeremiah*. Garden City, NY: Doubleday & Co., Inc., 1965.
13. Brown, Raymond. *The Epistles of John*. Garden City, NY: Doubleday & Co., 1982.
14. _____, et al. *The Jerome Biblical Commentary*. Englewood Cliffs, NJ: Prentice-Hall, Inc., 1968.
15. Buchanan, George Wesley. *To The Hebrews*. Garden City, NY: Doubleday & Co., 1972.
16. Caird, G. B. *Saint Luke*. London: Penguin Books, 1963.
17. Casey, Juliana. *Hebrews*. Wilmington, DE: Michael Glazier, Inc., 1980.

18. Conroy, Charles. *1-2 Samuel, 1-2 Kings*. Wilmington, DE: Michael Glazier, Inc., 1980.

19. Cowan, Marian, C.S.J., and John C. Futrell, S.J. *The Spiritual Exercises of St. Ignatius of Loyola: A Handbook for Directors*. New York: Le Jacq Publishing, Inc., 1982.

20. Dahood, Mitchell. *Psalms II, III*. Garden City, NY: Doubleday & Co., Inc., 1968, 1970.

21. de Mello, Anthony, S.J. *Sadhana, A Way to God*. St. Louis: The Institute of Jesuit Sources, 1978.

22. Dodd, C. H. The Parables of the Kingdom. New York: Charles Scribner & Sons, 1961.

23. English, John, S.J. *Spiritual Freedom*. Guelph, Ont.: Loyola House, 1974.

24. Erickson, Erik. *Childhood and Society*. New York: W. W. Norton and Co., Inc., 1963.

25. Fenton, J. C. *Saint Matthew*. Baltimore: Penguin Books, 1963.

26. Ferrucci, Piero. *What We May Be*. Los Angeles: J. P. Tarcher, Inc., 1982.

27. Fitzmeyer, Joseph. *The Gospel According to Luke I-IX*. Garden City, NY: Doubleday & Co., Inc., 1981.

28. Fleming, S.J. *The Spiritual Exercises of St. Ignatius: A Literal Translation and a Contemporary Reading*. St. Louis: The Institute of Jesuit Sources, 1978.

29. Ford, J. Massyngberde. *Revelations*. Garden City, NY: Doubleday & Co., 1975.

30. Fox, Matthew. *Breakthrough*. Garden City, NY: Image Books, 1977.

31. Getty, Mary Ann. *Philippians and Philemon*. Wilmington, DE: Michael Glazier, Inc., 1980.

32. Gill, Jean. *Images of My Self*. New York: Paulist Press, 1982.

33. Greenberg, Mosche. *Ezechiel, 1-20*. Garden City, NY: Doubleday & Co., Inc., 1983.

34. Hanson, James H. *Making Contact: Prayer in the Name of Jesus*. Minneapolis: Augsburg Publishing House, 1978.

35. Harrington, Wilfred. *Mark*. Wilmington, DE: Michael Glazier, Inc., 1979.

36. Heschel, Abraham J. *The Prophets.* New York: Harper and Row, Publishers, 1962.
37. Hitter, Joseph. "The First Week and the Love of God," *The Way*, Supplement 34 (Autumn 1978): 26-34.
38. Hughes, Gerard W. "The First Week and the Formation of Conscience," *The Way*, Supplement 24 (Spring 1978): 6-14.
39. Jung, Carl G. *Man and His Symbols.* New York: Valor Publications, 1964.
40. Kugelman, Richard. *James and Jude.* Wilmington, DE: Michael Glazier, Inc., 1980.
41. Kung, Hans. *On Being a Christian.* Garden City, NY: Doubleday & Co., Inc., 1976.
42. La Verdiere, Eugene. *Luke.* Wilmington, DE: Michael Glazier, Inc., 1980.
43. Leslie, Elmer A. *The Psalms.* New York: Abingdon Press, 1949.
44. Linn, Matthew, and Dennis Linn. *Healing of Memories.* New York: Paulist Press, 1974.
45. McBrien, Richard. *Catholicism Vol. I, II.* Minneapolis: Winston Press, 1980.
46. McKenzie, John. *Dictionary of the Bible.* Milwaukee: The Bruce Publishing Co., 1965.
47. McPalin, James. *John.* Wilmington, DE: Michael Glazier, Inc., 1979.
48. Magana, Jose, S.J. *A Strategy for Liberation.* Hicksville, NY: Exposition Press, 1974.
49. Maher, Michael. *Genesis.* Wilmington, DE: Michael Glazier, Inc., 1982.
50. Meier, John P. *Matthew.* Wilmington, DE: Michael Glazier, Inc., 1980.
51. Menninger, Karl. *Whatever Became of Sin?* New York: Hawthorn Books, Inc., 1973.
52. Miller, William A. *Make Friends With Your Shadow.* Minneapolis: Augsburg Publishing Co., 1981.
53. Mische, Patricia. "A New Genesis in Religious Communities and World Community," *Sisters Today* 53, no. 7 (March 1982): 387-398.
54. Ninehan, D. E. *Mark.* Baltimore: Penguin Books, 1963.
55. Osick, Carolyn. "The First Week of the Spiritual Exercises and the Conversion of St. Paul," *Review for Religious* 36, no. 5 (September 1977): 657-665.

56. Pennington, M. Basil. *Centering Prayer.* Garden City, NY: Image Books, 1982.

57. Perkins, Pheme. *The Johannine Epistles.* Wilmington, DE: Michael Glazier, Inc., 1979.

58. Pope, Marvin H. *Job.* Garden City, NY: Doubleday & Co., Inc., 1965.

59. Rahner, Karl. *Spiritual Exercises.* New York: Herder and Herder, 1956.

60. Reicke, B. *The Epistles of James, Peter and Jude.* Garden City, NY: Doubleday & Co., 1964.

61. Rollings, Wayne G. *Jung and the Bible.* Atlanta: John Knox Press, 1983.

62. Sanford, John A. *The Kingdom Within.* New York: Paulist Press, 1970.

63. _____. *The Shadow Side of Reality.* New York: The Crossroad Publishing Co., 1981.

64. Senior, Donald. *1 & 2 Peter.* Wilmington, DE: Michael Glazier, Inc., 1980.

65. Shakespeare, Wm. *The Complete Works of Wm. Shakespeare, Vol. 2.* Garden City, NY: Nelson Doubleday, Inc., n.d.

66. Speiser, E. A. *Genesis.* Garden City, NY: Doubleday & Co., Inc., 1964.

67. Stanley, David M. *A Modern Spiritual Approach to the Spiritual Exercises.* St. Louis: The Institute of Jesuit Sources, 1971.

68. Stuhlmueller, Carroll. *Psalm 1, Psalm 2.* Wilmington, DE: Michael Glazier, Inc., 1983.

69. Swain, Lionel. *Ephesians.* Wilmington, DE: Michael Glazier, Inc., 1980.

70. Taylor, Vincent. *The Gospel According to St. Mark.* New York: St. Martin's Press, 1966.

71. Teilhard de Chardin. *The Divine Milieu.* New York: Harper and Row, Publisher, 1960.

72. Veltri, John, S.J. *Orientations, Vol. I: A Collection of Helps for Prayer.* Guelph, Ont.: Loyola House, 1979.

73. _____. *Orientations, Vol. II: Annotation 19: Tentative Edition.* Guelph, Ont.: Loyola House, 1981.

74. Woodman, Marion. *Addiction to Perfection.* Toronto: Inner City Books, 1982.

To Our Readers:

It would be helpful to us, as we prepare to write the subsequent volumes of this series of guides for prayer, if you would be willing to respond to the following questions, and send your response to us.

    Thank You.

    Jacqueline
    Marie

_____

Please check the appropriate answers and add your comments.

1. I used the guide for prayer
    _____ regularly over a period of _____ (weeks or months).
    _____ irregularly.
    Comment:

2. I found the format (i.e., cover design, paper, type, layout)
    _____ helpful to my prayer.
    _____ unhelpful to my prayer.
    Comment:

3. I found the commentaries
    _____ helpful for entering into prayer.
    _____ difficult to understand.
    Comment:

4. The commentaries that were most helpful were on pages _____
    _____

5. I (used or did not use) the approaches to prayer.
    Comment:

6. What I liked best about the guide for prayer is _____
    _____
    _____

7. The following changes or additions would make the guide for prayer more helpful: _____
    _____

                     _____
                     (Signature optional)

Mail to Center for Christian Renewal at Jesuit Retreat House, 4800 Fahrnwald Road, Oshkosh, WI 54901.